D1252784

# A SHORT HISTORY OF
# ENGLISH RURAL LIFE

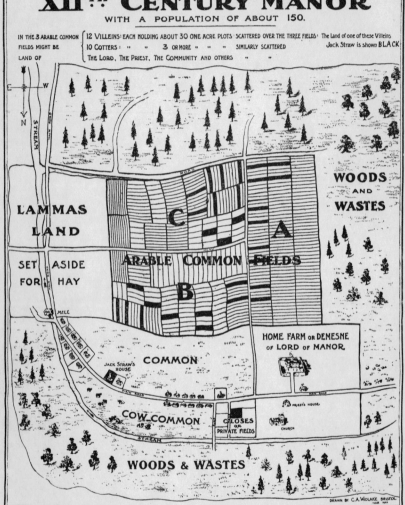

# PLAN SHOWING ARRANGEMENT OF THE LAND
## IN A
# XIITH CENTURY MANOR
### WITH A POPULATION OF ABOUT 150.

IN THE 3 ARABLE COMMON | 12 VILLEINS: EACH HOLDING ABOUT 30 ONE ACRE PLOTS: SCATTERED OVER THE THREE FIELDS: The Land of one of these Villeins
FIELDS MIGHT BE | 10 COTTERS: " " 3 OR MORE " " SIMILARLY SCATTERED | Jack Straw is shown BLACK
LAND OF | THE LORD, THE PRIEST, THE COMMUNITY AND OTHERS " "

WOODS AND WASTES

LAMMAS LAND

SET ASIDE FOR HAY

C

A

B

ARABLE COMMON FIELDS

MILL

COMMON

JACK STRAW'S HOUSE

HOME FARM OR DEMESNE OF LORD OF MANOR

COW COMMON

CLOSES OR PRIVATE FIELDS

PRIEST'S HOUSE

CHURCH

STREAM

WOODS & WASTES

DRAWN BY C.A. WIDLAKE BRISTOL

# A SHORT HISTORY OF ENGLISH RURAL LIFE

## FROM THE ANGLO-SAXON INVASION TO THE PRESENT TIME

BY

MONTAGUE FORDHAM, M.A.

TRINITY COLLEGE, CAMBRIDGE

WITH A PREFACE BY

CHARLES BATHURST, M.A., M.P.

AND A PLAN

LONDON : GEORGE ALLEN & UNWIN LTD.
RUSKIN HOUSE   40 MUSEUM STREET, W.C.
NEW YORK : CHARLES SCRIBNER'S SONS

*First published in 1916*

# PREFACE

To those—and they are now many—who are earnestly
seeking for a true solution of our many agricultural
problems, industrial, social and political, the study of
the conditions prevailing in rural England from the
earliest historical times and of the vicissitudes, both
of our greatest national industry and of the classes
engaged in it, is an indispensable equipment. By
such investigation alone can the difficulties of these
problems be appreciated, blunders in rural policy be
avoided, and antagonistic interests be reconciled. It
will be rendered easy and attractive by a careful
perusal of this little book, which skilfully summarizes
the chief features of English village life and English
agricultural history from Anglo-Saxon times down to
the XXth century. And a chequered and kaleidoscopic
history it is, replete with picturesque incident, remarkable in the vicissitudes of fortune of both rural industry
and rural population, and, as regards the peasant and
(more recently) the agricultural labourer, infinitely
pathetic and at times tragic. Round this pathetic figure

Mr. Montague Fordham sympathetically weaves his historical narrative. He pictures for us first the ancient self-governing village communities with their carefully partitioned open arable fields, their moots, their reeves and their haywards; then the feudal conditions of Norman times, based upon military organization, with their manors, demesnes, incidents of tenure and communal rights; the restlessness and misery of the XIVth century, with its Black Death and Peasant Revolt; the growing commercialism of the XVth and succeeding centuries, with its concomitant transition from customary tenants and bondsmen to tenant farmers and labourers: the continuous policy and process of enclosures, so fruitful in the economic development of England's agriculture, so fateful to the social development of England's peasantry; the growth of Puritanism in the XVIIth century and with it the disappearance of seasonal merrymaking and gaiety from the villages, and their replacement by religious rivalry and discord; the spread of sheep farming for cloth manufacture in the XVth and XVIth centuries, and that of more enlightened and economic methods of arable cultivation in the XVIIth and XVIIIth, the latter associated with the honoured names of Jethro Tull, "Turnip Townshend," Bakewell, Colling, Arthur Young and "Coke of Norfolk," when England was self-contained in the matter of her food supply and was pre-eminent among the nations of the world in her agricultural processes and prosperity : the disappearance of village industries, the waning of the leadership of the Church, and the rise of the country squire and the capitalist farmer in the XVIIIth and XIXth centuries : the periodical recrudescence during the last hundred years of emancipatory labour movements, headed by such sturdy countrymen as William Cobbett, Robert Owen and Joseph Arch : the improvements in agricultural machinery and rural science in the middle of the last century : and finally the catastrophe of the great agricultural depression which commenced in its late seventies, which ruined landlords, farmers and labourers alike and depleted the countryside both of men and money.

The writer lightly and hopefully touches upon the rural Renaissance of the XXth century, now rudely interrupted by the great European War. He rejoices, as all who really love their country must rejoice, at the improved amenities of village life, at the increasing facilities for a more rational system of education, and particularly at the spread of the Co-operative movement, invading, as it rightly does, every branch of agricultural activity, and not merely affording to the small-holder and allotment-holder the commercial advantages enjoyed by the larger farmer, but also welding together every class of the rural population in a common effort to promote the industrial welfare of the locality and to carry to the homes of the humblest of its workers a due proportion of the prosperity and happiness which such solidarity is bound to engender.

The old Squires of England were not always wise and were sometimes despotic, but they were, as a class, imbued with a traditional sense of honour, integrity, patriotism and sympathetic knowledge of their poorer neighbours which are not so markedly characteristic of the more progressive plutocracy which has largely replaced them.

The war will in its results afford unparalleled opportunities of awakening to new vigour the life of our villages and the development of a healthy, happy and largely increased rural community. The spirit of comradeship, self-denial, dogged courage and simple piety is abroad in the land, and is growing with every month of the present struggle for our national existence. It must be the aim of well informed rural reformers to turn this spirit to good account, and seek not by restriction, still less by penal legislation, but by mutual goodwill and sympathy to combine the freedom of life, social intercourse, innocent gaiety and simple religious faith of mediaeval rural England with an economic improvement such as that which marked the XVIIIth century, but one of which all classes alike will feel the benefit and by means of which the enterprising manhood of our villages will not decay while a surfeit of wealth accumulates in the hands of the few, but will find a ladder easy of ascent by which they may climb to a position of industrial independence and social advancement.

The inspiring "call of the land" will thus be heard and responded to by many of the most robust, physically and morally, of our fellow-countrymen and the stability of the nation enhanced thereby.

CHARLES BATHURST.

LYDNEY PARK,
*February* 1916.

# AUTHOR'S PREFACE

THE material on which this short history is based was first brought together for a series of lectures given to a group of villagers, who devoted many evenings in the winter of 1913–14 to the study of the history of country life. Any special quality that the book has attained is largely due to the discussions which took place on those winter evenings, in which men and women of all ranks of life and points of view took part. The lectures were a countryman's lectures, prepared for country people: but in the book I have considered also the needs of the student, to whom I believe my work will be found of use.

The history of English country life contains within itself the story of a number of little communities, each one differing from the others in the details of social, political and economic life. It is this wonderful variety that gives to the study of rural life its charm and interest. It is this same variety that creates difficulties for the historian. In this short history these difficulties are avoided to some extent by following only the main stream of events, thus securing a relatively simple story. There is another point of equal importance to be borne in mind. Rural history contains within itself the separate stories of two sections of society : the people with the control of power, and those who are controlled. A struggle between these two sections arose in very early times, and has never entirely died out. Sometimes, indeed, it burst forth into a storm, as for example when the peasants revolted against the upper classes in the XIVth century, and again when in the XIXth century poverty-stricken agricultural labourers combined into Trade Unions, and organized strikes for higher wages and better conditions.

I prepared the material with the greatest care, and have written in, I hope, a judicial spirit; but the history of the English countryside is a thorny subject, and I can hardly expect to escape criticism and perhaps correction. I welcome both.

I have only to make it quite clear that the book is not based on special original research, but on the writings of Prothero, Vinogradoff, Oman, Jusserand, Hasbach, Slater, Tawney, Sidney and Beatrice Webb, Cunningham and other recognized authorities.

Mr. Widlake of Bristol voluntarily prepared the large manorial plan from which the frontispiece of this book is reproduced: for the help I received from him and other members of my classes I desire to express my gratitude.

MONTAGUE FORDHAM.

RED CROSS BASE,
    BOULOGNE-SUR-MER,
      *February* 1916.

# CONTENTS

## PART I

### *MEDIAEVAL RURAL LIFE*

#### CHAPTER I

#### CHAPTER II

#### CHAPTER III

# CONTENTS

# CONTENTS

## PART II

# PART I

(About 450–1381)

## *MEDIAEVAL RURAL LIFE*

## CHAPTER I

### THE ANGLO-SAXON VILLAGE COMMUNITY

ENGLAND has, from very early times, contained within its boundaries corn-growing and pastoral districts, but corn-growing took in mediaeval times a much more important position than it does at the present day. Even in the earliest historic times, the corn crop had great importance. Indeed the invasion of the Romans, though to some extent a mere adventure, was certainly inspired, in part, by the desire to secure control of a country where not only was there mineral wealth, but also corn that could be exported. The Romans on their arrival in England found the country in the hands of the Celts, a race of the type of the Irish, a brave and imaginative people, with some civilization of their own which included a knowledge of such arts as the working of iron, copper and gold, and also apparently a love of music and poetry. Though there were even

*The Celts under Rome.*

1

in those days some small towns, the bulk of the population must have been occupied in hunting and agriculture and lived in small and scattered hamlets. They cultivated the land on some simple co-operative system, employing as a rule, in accordance with a custom common to many primitive nations, the method to be described hereafter of strip farming. Under the control of the Romans the country was developed, hard roads were laid out through the land, towns were built and the area under corn was greatly increased. As time went on Christianity and the civilization that accompanied Christianity spread, so that in the Vth century, when the Romans withdrew from Britain to defend their own country from Asiatic barbarians, much of the land must have been under cultivation, and a considerable section of the people were, it may be assumed, intelligent, and on the whole well-to-do.

Such was the condition of this island when towards the middle of the Vth century the Teutonic tribes, Jutes, Angles, Frisians and Saxons, our **The Anglo-Saxon invasion.** English ancestors, began to come across the North Sea. The first arrivals doubtless came on friendly missions, but when they found that the race who inhabited this country had, owing to many centuries of peace under Roman rule become unaccustomed to war, the newcomers must soon have formed the plan of making the fruitful fields of England their home. And as Asiatic barbarians began to push their way into their part of Europe, more and more of the tribesmen crossed over the ocean and spread through the country, driving before them the main body of the Celts, who retreated in some districts to the neighbouring hills, but generally to the more mountainous parts in the North and West of Britain. These newcomers were tough fighting farmers, pagan worshippers of Woden and Thor with none of the civilization of the Celts. They hung together in their families and tribes, fighting and ordering their lives in accordance with the ancient customs of their race.

It will be a help, in endeavouring to realize what actually occurred, to picture as definitely as we dare, the incidents in the advance of a party of these tribesmen. Let us take for illustration that section of the Jutes who, landing in the south of Hampshire, pushed their way up the Meon valley, driving before them the Celts who must have withdrawn to the hills above Petersfield, where to this day are found the scattered hamlets characteristic of Celtic rural life. An advance group of these immigrants, young men with their wives perhaps, might have found themselves in the district which afterwards became the XIIth century manor pictured in the frontispiece. Arriving in this valley, and crossing the stream at the point where the mill stood later, they would see immediately before them the remnants of a village which the Celts had deserted. On the left bordering the river, would be the fertile fields where later the meadows were plotted out, and in front the stretch of country, partly cleared, which in due time became the great arable fields. Here was a place suited for a settlement. Some rough huts would be quickly run up on the old Celtic site, near enough to the river to make it easy to fetch water, but yet far enough away to be above the mists and possible floods ; and then a barricade of wood or wattle, or perhaps a mud and flint wall, would be built round

*The creating of a village community.*

the hamlet as a protection from night attacks. Whilst this was being done, the man of the group who understood woodwork, the carpenter, would, with the help of the smith, be making a plough, or, more probably, putting into working order one left by the Celts. This done, the men, who might have brought with them or perhaps captured from the Celts the oxen they needed, would be in a position to begin the work of cultivation. A part of the open land on the southwest of the hamlet having been selected, the bush and rough grass would be burnt, so that the ashes might fertilize the soil, and the plough, which needed eight oxen to draw it, would be started by the appointed ploughman to plough each day a long narrow strip. Such a strip, of which one name a 'land'[1] is common at the present day, might also be called an 'acre,' a word that seems in early times to have meant a day's ploughing, varying in amount according to the nature of the soil and the custom of the locality. Between the ploughed acre strips would be left narrow belts of grass, a foot or so broad, to act as boundary divisions; and similar broader belts, to be used as rough roadways, would be left to edge the dozen or so ploughed acre strips that it was the custom to form into a group sometimes called a 'shot' or 'furlong.' When sufficient land had been ploughed, the various strips would be divided amongst the several families. The division might be made by lot, or perhaps the leader of the party undertook to make a fair partition. Whatever the arrangement, it was doubtless intended that every man should have a fair share in the land,

---

[1] Although this system was carried on throughout England, the names for the various features varied with the locality; see Appendix, p. 164.

having regard to the ever-changing quality of the soil throughout the fields. In the first year an area of land, part of that which afterwards formed the great common field marked A in the plan, might have been cultivated—50 acres perhaps : next year this land would be left to rest to renew its fertility and the ploughman would reclaim a fresh piece of land, part of the area B, to carry the corn crop. In the third year the ploughman would perhaps go back to A and plough up a piece there, and in the fourth year take a fresh piece from B. Then he might get to work again on the plots first ploughed in A and later in B, and so by degrees two great open fields of many strips grouped into shots would come permanently under the plough and be cultivated alternately. Each peasant family would under the custom obtain a number of strips, scattered in various parts of the fields, so that each might have a part of the good land and a share of the bad : and when the peasant family had harvested the crop, the land would fall back again into common use for all to feed their stock. Thus in a few generations, would be created great open arable fields, with scattered strips of the various peasant families. This arrangement, a main characteristic of the English village communities, prevailed in many places up to the XIXth century, and can be studied to-day at Laxton in Nottinghamshire, where it is still carried on in a modified form. Whilst the arable land was coming into use in this way, a similar arrangement was growing up for the grass meadows. Here again according to ancient custom, still prevailing at Yarnton in Oxfordshire, the land was divided into strips, and the right to mow and carry the hay was drawn for by the heads of the various

families. The hay once cut, the land fell back again
into common use and the stock fed over it. Usually,
a definite day was fixed on which arable or meadow
land became open to all. At Yarnton it was St.
Bartholomew's Day, but sometimes it appears that it
was Lammas Day, the first day of August of the Old
Calendar, the 12th of August of the present. 'Lammas
land,' a field-name common in the country at the
present day, is derived from the custom of throwing
open the land, whether arable or grass, on Lammas
Day.

As generations passed the village grew. The central
part of the valley would then be roughly plotted out,
part of the land becoming the village green for the
fowls, ducks and geese, and part a cow common. A
rough boundary to the tract of country that went with
the village would be marked out, and within that
boundary would lie stretches of woodland, into which
the villagers would drive their pigs and other stock
to feed on beech-mast, acorns and nuts. The tract
of land within this boundary would be the 'tùn,'[1] and
the people, the villagers, would be called the 'tùnsmen.'

Undoubtedly some such development created the
communities of East and West Meon and the neighbouring valley villages, which are of the clustered form
characteristic of the Anglo-Saxon settlements.

Whilst the people on the land were gathering into
their little communities and creating their
own laws and customs, the governing
class was organizing the kingdoms as a
whole; the features of this organization
that directly affected village life have now to be con-

The part
taken by the
governing
class.

---

[1] See Appendix, p. 163.

sidered.  England in the early days of the Anglo-Saxon period was ruled by a number of chiefs or kings, large and small, independent or tributary ; with them were associated their nobles, of whom the more important were the 'eorls' and the lesser were the 'thegns.'  The kings seem to have made it a practice to select some part of the land as their private estates, which were often scattered throughout the kingdoms.  In addition to this they claimed, by right of conquest, a control over the land they ruled.  This control was exercised it appears, in some districts, not so much by the kings and those attached to them as by the leaders of the groups that settled on the land.  It never amounted to private ownership as we understand it to-day, but took in time the form of certain definite rights.  These rights may for sake of distinction, since they appertained in the first instance to the rulers, be called 'the rulers' rights.'  Briefly, they were six :—

(1) The first was the right to tribute or services.  In earlier times this right was very varied.  In many cases it involved personal service, such as riding with messages, forming one of an escort, taking charge of the king's dogs or even teaching a king's daughter embroidery. More commonly the tribute took the form of corn or other food or of useful materials—a provender rent— thus an area of land might be subject to the duty of feeding the ruler and his retinue for a day and a night in every year, or to providing food for his dogs, or honey to sweeten his food and to make wax for his candles, or fleeces to be spun and woven into material for clothes.

(2) The second was a very important claim that all landholding men should conform to the 'trinoda necessitas' as it was called later, the famous *threefold*

*duty* of bearing arms, of repairing strongholds and of keeping bridges in order.

(3) Then there was the right to administer justice. This right appears as a rule to have been exercised in early days only by way of appeal from the democratic 'hundred' courts dealt with below; later on it was extended and became a valuable perquisite, for justice was a luxury and no one provided it free. It is true that trials took place under what was substantially a committee, got together for the purpose of the trial. This committee consisted of men of the litigants' own class, but the president of the court might be the king or someone who held under the king; and he, whilst conducting the proceedings, took at least a part of the fees and of the fines imposed on a wrongdoer.

(4) Further, there was the right to regulate markets and fairs and other forms of trading and fisheries, and to take tolls in relation to these matters.

(5) There was also a vague right akin to ownership, which seems to have held good, so long as the cultivators installed on the land were not interfered with. As a result a ruler or his representative could take over and cultivate, or colonize with his dependents, any land in the country districts not actually in use.

(6) Lastly there was the right, that did not apparently exist in early times, of levying king's taxes or 'geld.'

The kings, in place of retaining these rights in their own hands, proceeded in many cases to distribute them, reserving for themselves, as a general rule, the right to levy king's taxes, and also the right to claim from land-holding people the performance of 'the threefold duty.' In the earliest days grants of these rights were generally made, for the benefit of the Church, to a bishop, to a monastery, or to a religious community attached to the worship of a saint. A king on his conversion to Christianity, or maybe on repenting of his sins, would as the form ran 'for the love of Almighty God and his faithful servant Saint Peter' grant to a saint or to a bishop his rights over a score of tùns ; then the saint's representative or the bishop supervised the administration of justice, collected the tribute, overlooked the markets, and exercised the right akin to ownership over the surplus land, giving in return for these rights prayers for the soul of the king and his descendants. These grants were not made to the Church alone : the kings transferred the control of large areas of land to the great nobles, or eorls, whilst the supervision of smaller areas passed to the minor nobles, or thegns, men of the king's household or bodyguard. Such grants were made in return either for services rendered to the king or for promises of future support, and were in many cases subject to tribute or to other obligations. As a result very considerable amounts of landed property passed away from under royal control. Individuals who secured rights from a king distributed them from time to time amongst others, utilizing, perhaps, the old estate boundaries that may have prevailed since Roman times ; thus these rights came to be divided up amongst many persons, women, it may be noted, as well as men. At the same time, small plots of the unoccupied land were often handed over to such of the minor retainers of the kings or of the nobles or prelates as desired to retire from fighting to take up a farmer's life. Thus two new streams poured into the country from the upper class of people, enlarging the village communities : (1) a number of minor thegns and other retainers who took up small holdings, either as holders of definite plots of land or as sharers in the common fields and various rights ; and (2) a class of estate-holders, either bishops or other dignitaries of the Church, or eorls or thegns—soldier-squires ; these men had the control over the estates, as a rule large, lying either in one block or in scattered areas. These estate-holders not only possessed the rulers' rights of collecting tribute, administering justice, supervising markets and so forth, but they also in some cases took up land for their own personal use, so securing for themselves a home farm, the 'inland' as it was called, where they built barns and halls. From these centres they exercised control over the district, giving to the peasant farmers some measure of protection and support, and drawing from them in return something of the nature of a rent or tribute in food or military or other services. Though private property in land in the modern sense could hardly be said to have existed in those days, one can divide the land titles, so ar as they did exist, into two classes, the first based in origin on settlement confirmed by custom, and the second based on royal grant. This latter was called 'bok '—or book—land.

It is now possible to form some idea of the character of rural society and the nature of the village community, as it existed in the middle of the Anglo-Saxon period, before it had been modified through the growth of militarism and the increase of taxation. Society was at that time beginning to adjust itself into the form of a pyramid, with the workers on the soil at the bottom and the king at the top ; between were the eorls and thegns, bishops and other Church dignitaries, various steps in the

**The structure of rural life.**

social scale. Thus the men of a village community might live overshadowed by a small thegn or squire controlling perhaps 500 acres of land, to whom they rendered some slight services. The thegn might in his turn be the vassal of a great eorl or bishop holding half a county from the king. In some places the people still held from the king himself. In others the community was completely independent, for undoubtedly there were a large number of free villages and probably here and there unattached landholders dependent on no man. Such conditions of complete independence would, however, tend to disappear, as the estate-holders brought more and more of the people under their supervision.

The village community thus formed the bottom layer of society. This community made its home in a tract of land with roughly defined boundaries. **The village community.** As a rule this tract had its centre in a clustered village of from ten to thirty families, the typical Anglo-Saxon form ; but the farmhouses and cottages might be spread out in scattered hamlets, a form more characteristic of the Celtic race. Within the tùn's boundaries would sometimes be found the hall and home farm of an estate-holder, if there were one in the district ; but the most characteristic feature would be the great open arable fields already described, cultivated and fallowed alternately, the crops being wheat and rye, oats, barley and beans, and perhaps peas and tares. There were also 'lot meadows' divided into plots, and the pasture commons, the woods and the wastes for the use of all.

In their 'tofts'—farmhouses with farmyards and gardens—lived the farmers, either 'ceorls,' men of peasant origin, or small thegns and other men of military origin, all bound to take up fighting when called upon and to come armed with at least iron cap, shield and spear, to give battle for chief or king, whether in defence of the country or for warlike expeditions. Below these were a class of smaller holders, cottagers, and even a few slaves descendants in some cases of the Celts ; these men were liable to be called on to fight in time of dire need for the defence of the country.

After the VIth century, Christianity, taught by missionaries from Rome and by Celtic Christians, spread with its civilizing influence throughout the land, and ultimately there was found in every complete tùn the priest, a free man, and the 'tùn kirke,' the church of the community. The priests were expected to take a leading part in public affairs, and had even to fight for the country in time of necessity. They were supported in part by the gifts of the people, in part by tithes, which, however, in early days, appear in some cases to have been paid to the bishops : and also by the profits of land in the common fields, with which the village churches were very commonly endowed, through the piety either of the estate-holders or of the peasantry themselves.

The village communities were no mere jumble of people, but were well organized for local business ;

Local government. The moots.
this was dealt with, on democratic lines, by the 'moot' or village meeting, held sometimes in the church, but more commonly in the open air, either under the moot-tree or on the moot-hill. There such questions would be considered as the management of the common arable fields, the fencing of that part of the land on which

the hay and crops were growing, and the arrangements for ploughing and sowing, reaping and threshing; and there too would be decided the number of beasts, sheep and pigs that might be turned out on the common fields when not under cultivation, and the method of dividing up the lot meadows. The collection of the tribute of food, if such there were, would be settled at the moot and plans made for rendering services, if any, to the estate-holder and for providing the taxes. At such meetings the village officials were appointed. Of these the first was the reeve—who combined the duties of manager of the communal land and of a village mayor, for he supervised the agriculture and also presided at village meetings; he also, with the priest and four or more tùnsmen of good repute, represented the village in negotiations with outside authorities. Below the reeve was the 'hayward,' who under the direction of the former undertook, with perhaps the assistance of a 'field jury' or committee, the detailed management of the cultivation of the land. Amongst the other officials were the 'meadsman,' who saw to the division of the meadow-land, the 'woodreeve,' who looked after the woodlands and the ploughmen who ploughed for all. Finally there were the oxherds, shepherds, swineherds and beeherds, who looked after the oxen, sheep, pigs and bees. Without these men it would not have been possible to proceed with the Anglo-Saxon method of farming, which depended on the stock being in the hands of the herdsmen, and the peasant farmers being free to put in most of their time on the cultivation of the arable.

Although encroachments on boundaries, overcrowding the commons with beasts, and similar offences, had to be dealt with by the tùn moot, the punishment of

serious crimes that were committed in the village was
dealt with by the 'hundred,' a larger unit than the
tùn, being, it is thought, in origin a group of one
hundred families. The hundreds or 'wapentakes,' as
these were called in parts of East Anglia, held moots
or courts, which met from time to time to administer
justice. At this court leading landholders of the
district attended, and all or almost all judicial business
that arose in the hundred went first to it.

Whilst dealing with local government it is also
interesting to note that there was, in Anglo-Saxon
times, a shire or county moot. The shire moot, which
was in its character more aristocratic than the tùn and
hundred moots, met twice a year and dealt with county
business and legal questions relating to such matters
as land titles. Moreover, taxes imposed on the shire
were there divided amongst the hundreds, which in
their turn divided up the amounts placed upon them
amongst the tùns. The tùns were then bound to
collect and remit to the hundred the shares that were
imposed upon them, and the hundreds in their turn
remitted the funds so collected to the shire.

It is important to realize clearly that the country-
side was in those days already divided in accordance
with two different systems, out of which
The tùns and
the estates. sprang divisions which have lasted until
modern times. Of these two systems, the
typical features were: (1) the tùn or township, the
democratic village community, a unit somewhat of
the nature of a parish, and (2) the estates, large and small,
supervised by an eorl, a thegn, or a dignitary of the
Church, or in some cases by the king himself, a form
of organization represented later on by the manors

and their lords. Every tùn was regulated by its own customs, and every estate was managed in its own way ; there was no uniformity. Moreover, whilst most of the tùns were of the form described above, and were inhabited by the various classes of people already referred to, this was not always so. There were villages consisting of freemen of military origin, there were villages of peasant farmers only, and there were slave colonies working under the direction of a bailiff. The variation of character both in the estates and the village communities was, in early days, most marked in those parts of England where Celtic customs remained unchanged, and later on in the districts which were colonized by the Danes.

Conditions of life were always changing. The custom of dividing yearly the strips of arable land by lot disappeared in very early days, though **The develop-** in a few places it continued for many **ment of rural** centuries.[1] When it disappeared the **life.** peasant families would have had permanent occupation of their scattered strips, and whilst recognizing the rights that existed in most communities of grazing stock over all fallow land, they must have come to consider themselves owners of the land they occupied. Again, some of the larger farmers, as time went on, kept their own ploughs and teams and cultivated their land without having to resort to the common plough. Moreover, in some places, as generations passed and population grew, a third great open field would come into cultivation: then a new rotation would be introduced, every field in turn being cultivated in the

[1] In Gomme's "Village Community" a case of such annual redivision is mentioned as still occurring in the XIXth century.

first year with winter corn, wheat or rye, in the second with spring corn, barley, oats, beans or perhaps peas or tares, whilst in the third the land would be left fallow. And, with these minor variations, came the more important changes in the life of the people dealt with in the next chapter.

# CHAPTER II

## THE DEGRADING OF THE PEOPLE

THE Anglo-Saxons created a village life of their own, and this life, as time went on, gradually changed from its simple ways until at last in the XIth century it was forced into a new frame, the manor of the Norman times. As this change came the workers on the land were gradually pressed down, until at last the greater number of them were reduced to a condition of bondage. It should, however, be understood that this degradation was not merely the outcome of the Norman Conquest. In many places it must have begun at least two centuries before that event.

**The gradual depression of the people.**

In Anglo-Saxon times the degrading of the people arose from three main causes: (1) the distribution of the rulers' rights, (2) the growth of the military class and (3) the increase of the burden of taxation on the peasants.

**Causes of degradation in Anglo-Saxon times.**

The transfer to religious bodies or to private individuals of the kings' rights over the land was the first step in the degradation of the country people. Men of a distant village, provided with ample surplus land to feed their stock and to extend their arable or meadows whenever needed, rendering some

small tribute or service to the king and looking to him
for such justice as they could not administer themselves,
in their village meeting or in the hundred court, found
that the new holder of the rights took a far keener
interest in their lives than did his royal predecessor.
Should they wish to extend the arable or meadow land
to meet the requirements of an increased population,
the estate-holder had to be dealt with and some new
tribute or service might be claimed. If the men could
not arrange to extend the area of the arable land, the
holdings would have to be reduced in size all round, or
the younger men would find themselves without land
for their support. Many men thus squeezed out of
the community became the servants of the estate-
holders. Others similarly placed took some part of the
land that the estate-holder claimed, and the latter,
maybe, would provide them with stock on loan or on
lease; if they succeeded, all went well, but if they failed
they sank down still lower in the social scale. Again,
the village quarrel which the peasants could easily have
settled amongst themselves might, under the new conditions, be looked upon as a serious breach of the peace,
to be inquired into by the hundred court held under
the presidency of the holder of the profits of justice,
who took the fees and put into his own pocket the fine
that might have gone into the village chest and have
been spent for the good of the poor. In some cases the
supervision of justice by an eorl, bishop or other authority, which followed the alienation of the profits of
justice from the king, resulted in the setting aside of
the hundred moots and the creation of definite new
courts in their place. The informal village markets
must also at this time have become subject to stricter
supervision and to the exaction of tolls. Lastly, when

the estate-holder needed men to cultivate his land and could not obtain free labour, there is little doubt that men were forced to work for a certain number of days in the year on such of the land as he had appropriated for his own use.

The growth of military needs was a further cause of the degradation of the people. The constant struggles among the various Anglo-Saxon states, and the greater struggles between the Anglo-Saxons and Danes which went on intermittently in the VIIIth, IXth, Xth and even the XIth centuries, made regular armies a necessity. Soldiers more skilful than the old-fashioned Anglo-Saxon fighting farmers were required. Fully armed men on horseback, with lightly equipped men-at-arms, accustomed to war, were wanted, and the kings looked to the country estate-holders to supply their needs. The estate-holders were therefore on the look out for retainers to fight for them when required, and it became a common practice for men, otherwise free, to be attached to the estate or to the person of someone of higher rank than themselves. These bonds sometimes involved the men in the duty of working on their superior's estate, sometimes in performing other obligations, such as folding sheep on his land. In other cases they involved the definite duty, already referred to, of attending the superior's court of law and of acting as one of a committee of judges. The title of 'socman,' so common in the eastern side of England, seems to have arisen from this last custom, the word 'soc' or 'soke' usually implying, in early days, the duty of attending at a superior's court. But all men were not so bound, a large number being simply 'commended,' as it was called, to a superior. Such men appear to have been subject to one definite obligation only—to fight when needed. To be attached to a superior had certain advantages of real value in those troublous times, when a man's life and property were insecurely held. The men received their superior's support if their land title was questioned, if any attack was made on their personal liberty, or if prosecuted for crime; whilst, on his side, the superior was responsible for the good behaviour of his men. Hundreds of these attached men were to be found in Cambridgeshire. For example, in the village of Arrington, in King Edward the Confessor's time, there was one who owed allegiance to Eorl Waltheof; another who, whilst owing allegiance to, was also a member of the court of justice of the Abbot of Ely; a third was the man of 'Robert Wimarc's son,' and a fourth a servant of the lady called 'Edith the Fair.' It was through this custom of attachment that a feudal system began to grow, and with this growth the military men secured predominance amongst the peasant farmers and obtained larger holdings and probably the best of the land.

The effect on village life of the increased burden of taxation has also to be considered. It is easy to imagine that neither the kings nor the sheriffs, who in this matter represented them, would always find it convenient, after the distribution of royal rights, to go behind the local magnates in order to enforce the threefold duty on the men of the villages. And, in fact, the kings began to look more and more to the estate-holders to perform this duty, by providing knights and men-at-arms and by undertaking the repair of bridges and of strongholds. A division of responsibility then arose. The large estate-holders, eorls, thegns, bishops and others, undertook the provision of trained soldiers, while the duty of paying king's taxes fell on the peasant farmers. Thus the estate-holder's farm paid no taxes, whilst the rest of the land, the land in the hands of the peasant farmers, bore this burden. In early days the taxation, if any, appears to have been slight, the king relying on his tribute: but the people undoubtedly suffered after the appearance of the Dane Geld, a tax imposed at the end of the Xth century for the purpose of buying off the Danes, and continued from time to time, at first as a war tax, and later as an ordinary king's tax.

The conditions of life during the reign of Edward the Confessor can be pictured with the help of Domesday Book. Everywhere, or almost everywhere, were to be found the estate-owners, holding in many districts well-defined properties, including, as a rule, a home farm with its great barns for storing a tribute of food, and in some places a hall of residence. Below the estate-holders, within the village community itself, the classes described in the last chapter were still to be found, though their relative positions were slightly different. There were two distinct sections of cultivators: (1) the farmers of the upper class, who appear to have belonged, as a rule, to the military families. These men were called 'geneats,' 'drengs,' 'radmen,' and 'socmen'; they seem to have had a good position, holding perhaps 100 acres in the open arable fields, with a share of meadowland and rights over the commons. Such men were almost always attached to some superior, and they usually paid some definite rent or rendered military, or agricultural services for their land: if these services were agricultural, they were clearly defined and not excessive in amount. Moreover, they

*Conditions in Edward the Confessor's reign.*

were free men, and are so described in Domesday Book. Below these military and other free farmers were (2) the men of the old agricultural class, whose predecessors for some generations had been true peasant farmers, taking little part in fighting. Such men might be expected to be farming a 'yardland,' more or less, a holding consisting of some thirty acre strips in the open arable fields, with the corresponding meadowland and common rights. These men would render tribute in food to the estate-holder and might be bound by the obligation of working one or even two days a week on his home farm. In some cases they no longer owned stock, but hired it from the holder of the estate. The peasant farmers were not so free as the military farmers, though only serfs in the sense that they were forced to work. It was on these two sections of society that king's taxes fell. Below the peasant farmers were cotters, with five or so acres in the common fields, forced at that time, if agriculturists, to work on the home farm, if artisans, to render other labour services connected with their trade, such as making ploughshares or ox-yokes. Below the cotters were a few slaves.

Though these conditions were widespread, they were not universal. Life was somewhat differently organized in the East of England. The estates there often consisted of a small central property to which were attached rights of a varied character, extending over many independent men who might be living in many different villages. Moreover, in that part of England, a general state of freedom prevailed. This was largely due to the influence of the Danes, who, after some generations of fighting, had, by that time, settled down and colonized a large part of East Anglia.

In the winter of 1066 Edward the Confessor died.
Within twelve months Norman William was settled on
the throne, busily distributing the southern
half of England among his followers, whilst
a few years later he was dealing in similar
fashion with the North. The land titles of
the Anglo-Saxon eorls, thegns, bishops and other
estate-holders were cancelled and new grants were
made. These new grants can be divided into two
classes. To such of his Norman followers as were his
immediate vassals, or prelates whose influence he valued,
William made extensive grants: some men received
a score of estates, others half a county, whilst others
obtained merely a small plot of land. The greater part
of England was divided amongst such men. Then, to
certain of the English estate-holders who accepted the
Norman rule and swore allegiance to the king, their old
estates in their entirety or in part were re-granted,
either by the king or by his vassals. All estates were
created on feudal conditions. Every landholder was to
be the vassal of the king or of someone who held an
estate directly or indirectly of the king ; there was to be
' no land without a lord.' Moreover, the land was held
subject to good behaviour and a definite obligation to
provide a certain number of fighting men. Although
the tenure was a new tenure, and its leading features
spread through the arrangements made between all
sections of landholding society, William seems to have
intended that in the relations between the peasant
farmers and their immediate landlords, no new obligations were to be created ; the actual cultivators of the
land were not to be disturbed in their holdings or
position. He was shrewd enough to see that the wealth
and strength of the country depended on a contented

The invasion
of the
Normans and
its effect.

peasantry, living on good terms with himself and with the Norman lords, and able to provide a strong body of fighting men. Nevertheless, whatever the king's intention, the Norman Conquest came to the English peasantry as an overwhelming misfortune. In a large number of cases, the old Anglo-Saxon or Danish squire or other holder of the estate, belonging to the peasants' own race, with a knowledge of and respect for their customs, disappeared. He was replaced by a Norman, a man of foreign origin, who was not likely to be deterred by Saxon or Danish customs from obtaining from the peasantry sufficient tribute in food, in labour and in money to give him the wealth he required for his position. As a fact, the Norman lords proceeded to crush down the varied population living in the villages, reducing their rights and increasing their obligations. As a result many of the freemen were depressed into the position of the peasant farmers, and the peasant farmers and cotters were burdened with heavier tasks of labour. One simple example can be taken, to illustrate this point, from the record of Domesday Book. At Meldreth, a Cambridgeshire village bordering the upper Cam, there dwelt in the time of King Edward the Confessor 15 socmen, freemen, possibly of Danish origin; 10 of these men were vassals of the Abbey of Ely and seem to have had between them some 300 acres of land, probably the fertile land that lies by the river, whilst the others, holding between them about half that area, were the men of a Saxon Eorl Aelfgar. After the Conquest a Norman lord took over the Meldreth estate and created out of it a manor for himself. He appropriated some land for his home farm, and for that he must have needed labour. He could have given little consideration to the claims of the socmen. It is, indeed, definitely known that they were degraded, since the Domesday record tells that, twenty years later, the Meldreth estate consisted of the home farm of the lord and outlying peasants' land, and the population comprised one slave and eighteen cotters, labourers, apparently, with small holdings, the descendants of the old freemen of the village. This story well illustrates what went on throughout England. The new lords took a firmer grip on the land and people, determined that both should be organized, not in the easygoing Anglo-Saxon way, but on the business basis of the manor. The people were to work harder for their new masters.

During the first century of the Norman rule, arduous feudal conditions were being introduced by the kings in their relation to their immediate feudal tenants. The marriages of children were controlled, and fines or payments exacted. Then a right of wardship was enforced, giving the king an opportunity of taking over and managing, largely for his own profit, the estates of minors. Corresponding exactions were in turn introduced by the king's tenants into the arrangements with their own sub-tenants, and so on from class to class of feudal holders, until finally heavier burdens came on to the shoulders of the peasants themselves. During the same century there was introduced the custom called 'astriction,' by virtue of which such of the peasantry as were not of the class of freemen were bound to remain in their homes. As a result of these further changes, the position of the peasants became definitely worse, whilst such genuine grievances as they had were rarely remedied in the national courts, since these courts made it clear that they would only interfere in manorial matters as between the lord and the freemen, and refused any relief to the lower class of the peasantry. Nevertheless, in considering the condition of the people it is well to realize that it was against the interest of the lords to grind them too hard, for the lords had to maintain a sturdy peasantry, able to fight for them if needed. There is, indeed, good reason to suppose that in many places the position of the villagers was still tolerable. Especially would this be so in districts controlled by the king himself, or by a bishop or other Church dignitary, and in outlying villages where the lord or his steward rarely came.

Whilst the Norman lords installed by William as landholders were organizing their estates into the manorial form, the king, who needed money to carry **Domesday Book.** on the state, decided to put a tax on the land of England at the rate of 6s. on the 'hide.' The hide is a word of varied meaning, but it usually implies an area of 120 acres. The tax therefore worked out at one halfpenny an acre of cultivated land ; perhaps a quarter of the annual value. The lords claimed that by custom the peasants' land alone paid king's taxes, and probably also gave too low statements of the area under cultivation. In any case, William was not satisfied with the results of the levy, and he decided to have an investigation into the amount of land available for taxation. He therefore ordered in the winter of 1085–6 that a record of the condition of rural England should be prepared. Land commissioners went to every county, and from every tùn came the tùn's representatives, priest, reeve and six tùnsmen, to meet the commissioners and to tell the story of their village. These delegates were called upon to give the names of their lord and his estates, to report on the area of his home farm and the number of plough teams he had ; they had also to tell of the area of the land held by the peasantry and of their plough teams, and as to what woods, meadows, pastures, mills, fisheries and markets there were. They were then asked for similar information of the conditions of their village in Edward the Confessor's reign. Besides this, they had to give the number of unfree peasant farmers (at that time as a rule called 'villeins' and looked on as serfs), of cotters (also considered as serfs), of slaves, and also to report if there were freemen. The information so gathered was doubtless checked by reference to the representatives of the hundreds and of the Norman colonists, who were bound to attend the meetings of the commissioners. It was then recorded by the commissioners. These collected records form Domesday Book.

Three of these entries, giving a picture of three properties, follow : they have been translated somewhat freely.

(1) At Limpsfield (in Surrey) there are on the home farm 5 plough teams : there are also 25 villeins and 6 cotters with 14 teams amongst them. There is a mill worth 2s. a year and one fishery, a church and four acres of meadow, wood for 150 pigs and two stone quarries, each worth 2s. a year, and two nests of hawks in the wood, and ten slaves. In King Edward's time the estate was worth £20 a year, afterwards £15, now £24.

(2) The king holds Lovecomb (in the Isle of Wight). Sawin, a Saxon thegn, held it in King Edward's time, free from all service except a land tax ; it was then assessed for taxation as a hide, now for two-thirds of a

virgate.[1] There is one ploughland in the home farm, on which work 6 cotters and 2 slaves. In the time of King Edward, the king's tribute had been computed and was paid at the rate of £4 a year; the estate is now worth but £3 a year and yet the king draws £4 from it.

(3) Here (in Herefordshire) in the midst of the woodlands, and outside the district of any hundred, lives a solitary farmer. He owns a plough team of eight oxen and has his own plough. Two serfs help him to cultivate the hundred or so acres that he has reclaimed. He pays no taxes and is the vassal of no man. There is also a Welshman living here, with a little holding for which he pays three shillings a year.

Domesday Book does not deal with the whole of England; a few counties in the North, Northumberland, Cumberland, Westmorland and Lancashire, and Monmouth on the Welsh border, are not included, but within the area of inquiry the information is fairly ample.

Authorities report that the total population recorded in Domesday approximately consists of:—

(1) 9,300 tenants in chief and under-tenants, that is to say nobles, ecclesiastics and others holding large and small estates on feudal tenure.

(2) 35,000 socmen and other freemen, almost all of whom are found in the north-east of the area dealt with.

(3) 108,500 peasant farmers, here called villeins, distributed fairly evenly throughout the area.

(4) 89,000 cotters similarly distributed; and

[1] The virgate is the Norman name for the Anglo-Saxon yardland.

(5) 25,000 slaves, almost all of whom were to be found south of a line running from the mouth of the Wash to the north of Hereford, the area in which, 800 years later, the worst paid and worst housed labourers were to be found.

Domesday Book could hardly have covered the ground completely, and it will not be an excessive estimate to suggest that there were 300,000 heads of families living in the area under consideration. These heads of families must have represented as many as 900,000 individuals working on the land, for wives and children would certainly have taken their share in the labour. This, it is interesting to know, does not greatly differ from the number of persons engaged in agriculture in the same area at the present day.

The amount of land under cultivation is not clearly given and cannot be stated with any certainty; but some authorities think that there were 9 million acres of land under the plough, of which less than two-thirds would bear crops in any one year. At the present time there are about 10 million acres of arable in the same counties. There was, in addition, meadow land, perhaps a million acres in all, and a large area of pasture commons and of woods and wastes. In the same counties there are found to-day, some 12 million acres of pasture and meadow land.

It is easy, with the help of Domesday Book, to picture the Normans busily engaged in the reconstruction of English country life, throwing estates together, adjusting boundaries, and thus forming, wherever possible, convenient units, and then collecting into the hands of the owners of those units the control of justice, of markets, and of other similar rights.

# CHAPTER III

## THE MANOR AND THE VILLAGE

IN the XIIth and XIIIth centuries, the manorial system prevailed in England, built up by the Normans on the foundations of the old estates, a structure forming a wall and roof, as it were, over the democratic English village communities. In these centuries England may, then, be pictured as divided up into little manorial kingdoms, in the main self-supporting, each with its own governor—the lord of the manor—and its own rules and customs. In some cases the manor would take the form of a number of small or large holdings lying in many places, a widely scattered estate; in others, the manor stretched over a great area, like the Bishop of Winchester's manor of East Meon in Hampshire, with its fifteen tithings or village communities and 24,000 acres of land within its boundaries, while some manors extended to twenty or thirty acres only. But the manor in its most characteristic form would be a compact area coinciding with the 'vill,'[1] as the village community was called at that time. Manors were often divided one from another by broad stretches of woods and waste lands, or perhaps by great forests in royal ownership, while the roads by which they

*General character of the manors.*

[1] See Appendix, p. 163.

were connected would, unless of Roman origin, be
of the roughest description—mere broad grass tracks,
deeply furrowed by the wheels of carts and the feet
of cattle—often impassable in winter save for horses
and foot passengers.

The manor as it existed at this period, though
elaborate in form, was a straightforward organization,
well suited to the needs of the period and not unadapt-
able to the changes of time. The description which
follows will, it is hoped, make its general character
clear to the reader, who will be helped, in this analysis,
if he refers to the plan given as a frontispiece to this
book.

The buildings of a manor of any size would be:
The Hall and Barns and other buildings of the
Home Farm, the property of the lord of
**The buildings.** the manor; the Mill, also as a rule his
property; the Church, the Priest's House,
and the small farm-houses and cottages with their
outbuildings that formed the Village.

Outside the village would be the enclosed part of
the lord's farm, and in some cases one or two detached
farms, hired or owned by independent
**The land.** farmers, and a few small closes for young
stock. Then there would be all that remained of the peasants' land of the Anglo-Saxon period,
by that time bound into the manorial estate and
controlled by the lord, but still occupied by the peasant
farmers and cotters—men of Anglo-Saxon or Danish
origin—and cultivated by them in accordance with
the ancient customs of their race. The characteristic
features of this part of the manorial estate would be

little, if at all, changed from what had existed before the Conquest.   There would still be :—

(1) *The open arable fields*, either two, or more commonly three great areas, fenced either permanently or temporarily from the surrounding land.   These fields would consist of many hundreds of strips, the 'acres' or 'lands,' the divisions between the strips being marked by the old narrow grass belts, the 'baulks,' or in some cases by deep furrows.   The 'lands' would be still, as they had been in the past, grouped together and surrounded by broad grass headlands or rough grass roads, the 'headlands' and 'way baulks,' so as to form divisions or fields, the 'shots' or 'furlongs.'

(2) *The Lot Meadows*.—Land set aside for hay, and divided either permanently or yearly into strips.

(3) *Commons*.—Much larger in extent than the areas that bear that name to-day, and consisting in part of valuable pasturage for stock and in part of rough land.

(4) *Woods and Wastes*.—Wood and moor land, hillsides and marshes, open to all the village.

The social organization of the manor has next to be outlined.   At its head was the lord, whom Norman **The people** law inclined to look upon as the owner of **and their** the land as well as a governor of the **social or-** estate.   The lord might be the king, a **ganization.** monastery, or other ecclesiastical institution, a bishop or some other Church dignitary, or a layman, either some Norman noble holding many such estates, or perhaps merely a modest squire, holding a few manors, or one only.

Such manors would rarely, if ever, be bought and sold.   If they were vested in the Church, they would remain in the hands of the Church, whilst if a manor were in lay hands it would, in the ordinary course, pass from father to son, remaining in the same family for many generations, unless it happened that the manorial lord broke some feudal rule that caused his land to escheat to and become vested in his superior. In such cases it would be re-granted to some new owner to hold on similar feudal terms as his predecessor. Not only were such new grants made of old manors, but new manors were created by the grant of the lord of a manor of some part of his estate specially allotted. This practice of so creating new manors ceased in the year 1290.[1]

Few of the greater lords would be found in those days permanently residing in any particular manor, and in their absence the representative would be a seneschal, a land agent or lawyer steward, who would supervise several manors, having under him a bailiff for each estate.

There might be, in a manor, a few free farmers, socmen[2] and other freemen. These men had a privileged position, and stood between the lord and the lower class of farmers, often acting as a barrier to the encroachments of the former on the common and other rights. Some freemen held their land on quite trivial or nominal services, others continued, as had their predecessors of the past, to hold their land subject to clearly defined obligations, either military or religious, or, if agricultural, of a superior kind, such as attending with their ploughs on certain days in the year to plough parts of the lord's lands. This class was not large in number, save in parts of the north-east of England. The main body of the farmers were no longer free but definitely 'bondsmen,' and as such subject to the rule

[1] See Appendix, p. 176.  [2] Ibid., p. 163.

of the lord and his bailiff; nevertheless they would hold doggedly to such old customs as had not been destroyed in the years directly following the Conquest.

At the head of the peasants was still the reeve, at that time sometimes called the 'provost' or 'praepositus,' titles introduced by the Normans; below the reeve there was still in most manors the hayward to manage the husbandry, and in some manors a meadsman continued to look to the meadows, a wood-reeve to supervise the woods, whilst a beadle collected rents; in large manors other officers might be found.

Of the bondsmen there were two main groups, somewhat similar to the two classes of non-military peasant farmers that lived in the villages before the Conquest. The 'villeins,'[1] as the Normans nominated the unfree peasant farmers of the upper section, formed the larger of these groups. The extent of their land varied, but thirty acres in the open field was the typical villein's holding. The second group, the cotters, as it is convenient to call them, held less land than the villeins, five acre strips being about the average.

Amongst the peasantry were men who had special positions in the village life, oxherds, shepherds, swineherds, gooseherds and beeherds, engaged in looking after the oxen, sheep, pigs, geese and bees. With them may be grouped such men as the thatchers, the village ploughmen, and the ackermen or drivers of oxen. These men were in a sense officials, and worked

---

[1] The title 'villein' is often used in contemporary and modern writings to describe the bondsmen, that is, the peasants of the classes that lay between the freemen and the slaves; it has in this book been limited to the class that lay between freemen and the cotters, in accordance with the division as a rule made in Domesday Book.

for both the bondsmen and the lord, and also perhaps for the independent farmers, if there were any in the manor.

There were also craftsmen in the village, for a community of this character, which had to be largely self-supporting, could not progress without workers able to make the ploughs and carts and other agricultural implements, the shoes and articles in leather, and to weave materials for the clothes. There were therefore in the village communities blacksmiths, workers in wood, leatherworkers, and weavers. These craftsmen then, as ever since, appear to have taken a leading position in village life.

From early times there were also to be found in many villages a few landless labourers, a small class that persistently increased generation after generation.

Although there might be men among the herdsmen and the artisans who were free, and others who were slaves, this was probably exceptional; the mass of the village population usually belonged to the intermediate class, the bondsmen.

In addition to the men of the village community there were, in most manors, some servants of the lord, amongst whom were perhaps ploughmen, carters, and herdsmen who worked for the lord alone, and in some places there were slaves—a diminishing class. These servants and slaves usually lived in the precincts of the manorial hall.

Before dealing with the general character of the life in the manor, it is convenient to give a short account of the government of the manorial estate and the underlying community.

**Local government.**

The village community, the vill, still continued in these centuries as a definite public body.

There was no official corresponding to the steward of a manor to record the rights, duties and acts of the vill, and as a consequence comparatively little is known of its constitution and character. But it is clear that it was a unit subject to taxation, and was responsible for order, whilst vills appointed at least one executive officer, the constable, who dealt with these questions. The vill continued to be represented in the hundred court and in negotiations with outside bodies by the priest, reeve and selected responsible villagers. The powers and duties of the village community, although they continued, were probably less important than they had been in earlier days or became in later centuries.

The more important minor authority at that time was the 'halimoot,' a court of the manor that came into existence in the XIth or XIIth century, and lost much of its power and importance after the XIVth. This moot or court assembled, usually, every three weeks and holders of land in the manor were bound to attend. Its natural place of meeting was the manorial hall; though in some villages an old custom prevailed of holding meetings in the open air. At this court certain offences were dealt with— bad ploughing, the breaking down of fences, the flight of a peasant from his manor, and such misdemeanours were punished; whilst in some manors more severe crimes were judged—for example, a thief might have to be tried and perhaps condemned to death. Further than this, questions of the rules and customs of the manor were here settled: the introduction of a new tenant on the death of his predecessor, the right of a widow to dower, the transfer of land, the rents, services and obligations of the tenants and their relations with the lord, all came before this court and were adjusted from time to time. The lord of the manor or his representative acted as the president of the court, but the peasantry were the judges, and in practice decisions were often left to an appointed committee or jury of six or twelve men. Notwithstanding the fact that in this court the decisions rested with the peasantry, it is important to realize that the absence of any effective right of appeal against arbitrary action of the lord must have given him a predominant influence in all questions that affected his rights and duties.

It does not appear that the actual management of the husbandry was settled by the halimoot. In large manors containing many communities, such a course could hardly have been followed. It is probable that a 'foreman of the fields' and field juries were appointed by the peasants to look after open arable fields and commons, working in conjunction with the bailiff, hayward and other officials; and, where there were many communities within the manor, there may have been a corresponding number of such foremen and juries.

The other local courts were the hundred moot and the shire moot, inherited from Anglo-Saxon times, and various courts of a feudal character ; these latter courts were founded by the owners of the profits of justice, and competed in the administration of judicial business with the older democratic courts, which, indeed, they sometimes superseded.

With these facts clearly understood, it is not difficult to get an idea of the general character of a manorial estate. The hall or manor house, detached

from the village, was the centre of its own life. It
consisted as a rule of a large hall, with one or two
smaller rooms; near by would be the court-
yard with a barn for storing corn, a dove-
cot, farm buildings and possibly rooms for
farm servants and slaves. Then there would
be a garden with fruit trees and vegetables, and often a vineyard. With the hall went the
home farm, the land of the Anglo-Saxon estate-
holder extended and called the 'demesne.' It would,
in all probability, consist of a few enclosed fields
near the hall with a considerable number of strips
intermingled with the peasants' strips in the open
fields, and held subject to the same rules as the
peasants' land. The possession of these strips would
therefore carry with it a share in the lot meadows,
and a proportionate share in the rights over commons,
woods and wastes.

*Some general characteristics of the estate.*

Unless the manor happened to be in the hands of
a small resident squire, it would be the seneschal or
the bailiff who would reside at the hall. But now
and again the lord of the manor would come with
his retinue of servants and retainers to visit his estate.
The life on such occasions would be rough and
simple : the retainers would camp in the big hall or
in the outbuildings, taking meals in the former, and
sleeping there on bundles of rushes, fern or straw.
The lord would reserve for himself and family the
private room or rooms, but would join his retainers
in the hall for meals. The lord, whose interests lay
in the main in outside affairs and not in husbandry,
might be expected to stay for a month or two of
every year in the manor, until he had consumed a
large proportion of the stores of food, gone through

the bailiff's accounts and enjoyed some days' sport in the woods and wastes. This done, he would be off to another estate.

An important element in the manorial life was the mill. If, as was a common custom, it belonged to the lord, he would claim the right to grind the corn grown in the manor, so that every bondsman and perhaps even the freemen, had to come to the lord's miller, who, holding a monopoly, probably often charged undue prices, and so taxed unfairly the people's small gains.

Important, though in a different way, were the church and the church house. The church was not only a religious, but also a social centre, and in it were often held meetings, plays and even markets. But commonly the village life centred in the church house, where the village priest may have lived. Though simpler than the lord's hall, this house would be built on the same plan, with one large room, suitable for business and social meetings of the villagers. The priest continued to be an important official in the community, taking his part not only in the religious but also in the social and public life. For his services he received burial and other dues, a share of the tithes, and also the gifts of his flock, whilst he would generally, like his Anglo-Saxon predecessor, hold several strips of land in the open fields.

In the village itself, which might straggle along a rough lane, littered with refuse, would be the small farm-houses of the peasants. The ordinary type of farm-house would contain one large room common to all. Above this room might be a loft, reached by a ladder. Most of the houses would be, of their kind, well built, for there is no reason to suppose that an

English peasant did not have the intelligence to build himself a wind and weather proof house. Materials would come from the woods and wastes, where ample timber was, in most manors, to be had for the cutting. The walls of his home might be of logs, or of wattle daubed with clay, or of rough stones like an old-fashioned Irish cabin, or of clay bats or clunch or turf, according to what was procurable in the locality. The roof would be thatched with reeds or straw. There could have been but little furniture in such a house, the only household belongings of the peasant of any value being his cooking pots. Brushwood, fern or straw would serve for beds. A wood fire would burn in the centre of the room, from which the smoke would find its way through a hole in the roof. Round the house would be a yard, some outhouses and perhaps a garden : this little holding might still, as in Anglo-Saxon times, be called a toft, a name still in use at Laxton. Such a toft would be occupied by a freeman or a bondsman. The former might perhaps have an enclosed farm of his own, but such a condition was probably rare, and the freeman's holding would approximate to the villein's now to be described ; the difference between the condition of freeman and bondsman lying, not in the nature of their land, but in the fact that freemen's obligations were less arduous than bondsmen's, whilst the freemen were not astricted and their rights were protected by the national law. The extent of the villeins' holdings varied in the same manor, and in this, as in almost all other details, the holdings differed in one manor from another. But every villein toft-owner would have a definite holding that went with the house. This holding, if of the ordinary type, would consist of—

(1) A certain number of scattered strips divided amongst the open arable fields. These strips were cultivated for the peasant's private advantage from the time that the land was ploughed until the crop was off, after which the strips would in most manors revert to common use for all to feed their stock.

(2) The right, enjoyed in most manors by freemen and villeins only, to the hay crop on one or more strips in the lot meadows, for which, in accordance with ancient custom, an annual ballot would take place.

(3) The right to feed cattle, oxen, horses, sheep, pigs and fowls on the commons and in the woods and wastes, also over the lot meadows when the hay was cut, and as a rule, in addition, over the arable land when crops were off. This right must have carried with it a claim on the services of the village herds-men.

(4) A right to get from the woods and wastes, wood for firing and building and for making fences and tools, and also turf and stone or sand and other similar material.

(5) The right, contested perhaps by the lord of the manor, but enjoyed nevertheless, to catch game on the same area; this was a great privilege when winter food was short.

And lastly, the peasant, if fortunate, would have—

(6) A small private close for the use of his young stock.

The plan of a manor which forms the frontispiece of this book shows, so far as is possible, the various features and gives the holding of a typical villein, Jack Straw, marked in black. This manor is one containing a single village. In it the farming is presumed to be carried on upon the three-field system, and Jack Straw holds, it will be observed, ten acres in each field. This thirty-acre farm was the normal villein's holding.

The peasants, whether freemen, villeins or cotters, must have felt that the strips of land in the open arable fields and the lot meadows were their own, and that the commons, woods and wastes belonged to the community, basing their claim on ancient custom. The Norman lord on the other hand, since his ancestors and their king had conquered the land, claimed that the soil of the whole estate was his, and that, whatever the title of the freemen, the bondsmen, at any rate, had no definite rights, but held their fields, as the phrase ran, 'at the will of the lord.' The difference between the peasantry on the one hand claiming as the descendants of the original settlers, and the lords claiming by right of conquest—a quarrel inherited in part from Anglo-Saxon times—continued through the manorial period and led to much friction. The law, as before explained, recognized the freemen as having a legal title to their land and common rights, but gave the lord a right to enclose woods and wastes not required by the peasantry, a right explained and defined by the Statutes of Merton and Westminster.[1] Further than that the law supported the lord of the manor as against the bondsmen, since until the end of the XIVth century the national courts of justice would not, as before mentioned, interfere to give protection to a bondsman who was being evicted or otherwise evilly treated in matters relating to his land holding by his lord. The bondsman was in the eye of the law the subject of the lord, and so interference was not logical.[2] But, what-

_Land tenure and the law._

[1] See Appendix, p. 168.     [2] But see Appendix, p. 163 (B).

ever the view of the law, custom was powerful, and the interest of the lord often went with it, for he naturally wished to keep on good terms with the men on whose help he relied both in peace and war. The bondsmen's families, therefore, must have had in a large number of cases what amounted to permanent tenancies, the land passing, generation after generation, from father to son.

For their holdings the peasants, whether free or bond, rendered various agricultural services or rents. These services and rents fall under three main headings: (1) Week-work, an obligation which compelled the peasant to work a certain number of days per week on the lord's land. (2) Boon-work, which compelled him to undertake special work, as, for example, carting corn to market for the lord. (3) 'Gafol,' a tribute in cash or kind, such as a hearth penny per year, or a dozen eggs at Easter, or corn or honey, or young stock, fish or fowls. Bondsmen had also sometimes to pay, in addition, taxes at the lord's discretion.

These services and rents varied not only in the different manors, but in the various sections of the community. Freemen's obligations were comparatively light, and it appears that the freeman had never to undertake the week-work ; villeins', which were heavier, were different from cotters', while artisans' and herdsmen's varied from the true peasant farmers'. Moreover, the obligations of the men of the same section varied with their holdings. A specimen of an Oxfordshire villein's services—a thirty-acre man—as rendered in the XIIIth century, is given in illustration.[1]

[1] This information, which is to be found in the Hundred Rolls of Edward I, is based on the extracts from the Rolls given in the late Mr. F. Seebohm's invaluable book on "The English Village Community," pp. 43-4 (Longmans).

### Week-work.

| | Valued at |
| --- | --- |
| | s. d. |
| From 2 to 3 days' work a week : a total of 122½ days' work in the year ... ... ... ... | 6 9 |

### Boon-work.

| | s. | d. |
| --- | --- | --- |
| Six days' special work with one man ... ... | 1 | 0 |
| One day's reaping with two men, food provided | 0 | 2 |
| 'Half a carriage' for carrying wheat and the same for carrying hay ... ... ... ... | 0 | 2 |
| Ploughing and harrowing one acre ... ... | 0 | 6 |
| A ploughing called 'graserthe' ... ... ... | 0 | 1½ |
| One day's harrowing of oatland ... ... | 0 | 1 |
| Making a quarter of malt... ... ... ... | 0 | 1 |
| One day's washing and shearing sheep ... | 0 | 0½ |
| One day's hoeing ... ... ... ... ... | 0 | 0½ |
| Three days' mowing ... ... ... ... | 0 | 6 |
| One day's nutting ... ... ... ... ... | 0 | 0½ |
| One day's carrying to the stack... ... ... | 0 | 0½ |
| Total ... | 2 | 9½ |

| | s. | d. |
| --- | --- | --- |
| Gafol.—Horse load of wood ... ... ... | 0 | 0½ |

Taxes.—Tallage : once a year at the lord's will.

It will be seen from this example that the gafol or tribute was not very heavy ; indeed the claim on the man's time was everywhere the most serious demand, especially at harvest, when there must often have been a struggle between the bailiff and the men for the labour necessary to get in the crops. But apart from these special times the bondsman could hardly as a rule have been greatly overworked, for though he certainly laboured for long hours in the summer the Church saw that he had his Sundays and saints' days free ; and saints' days were so numerous that he must have had on an average one 'holyday' a week.

The bondsmen of the second rank, the cotters, either held a plot of land with their cottage or else a few acres, averaging perhaps five, in the common field. These men differed from the villeins in that it was rare for them to have oxen, but they certainly had other stock, and held with their land the usual rights over the commons, woods and wastes, though they do not seem to have shared in the lot meadows. Their services were less in amount than those of the villeins. For example, a Cambridgeshire cotter holding an acre of land, was only bound to provide his manorial lord with a hen at Christmas and five eggs at Easter, and to do a day's work on Monday in each week ; whilst if Monday happened to be a festival he was freed for that day from his obligation.

The herdsmen, ploughmen, etc., rendered for their land services in looking after the stock, or in ploughing the land or in performing similar duties ; whilst the artisans would pay by work done in their crafts or trades.

The character of the bondsmen's tenure, and the services, whether traditional or imposed by Norman lords, were as time went on entered in **Manorial records.** manorial records. The recording of titles was of benefit to those tenants who had better rights than the mere holding 'at the will of the lord' ; for their rights were set down on their entry into their holdings, and it became a custom towards the middle of the XIIIth century to supply the tenant with a copy of the record of such entry or 'admission.' These men so supplied with a copy of the record are later on described as copyholders. But the recording of services was looked on with suspicion by the peasantry. They could, indeed, have had very little voice in preparing these records and must have constantly doubted their accuracy. It is interesting to note that in the rising in 1381 the manorial records were, we are told, constantly searched for and destroyed by the peasants.

In considering the position of all the peasants below the rank of independent farmers, it is important to remember that their serfdom involved them in many serious restrictions. These men were at that time astricted: they belonged to the estate, so that a bondsman had no right to leave the manor in which he lived without the lord's consent. Indeed, so long as the lord depended on forced labour for the cultivation of his land, for which he in his turn had to provide some form of rent or tribute, or render services to the king or to his feudal superior, he could not very well allow the villeins and cotters, the workers on his land, to leave at their pleasure ; he might then soon be without labour to work his land, and thus unable to discharge his own duties and obligations. Men did, however, arrange to leave in some cases, and then a special tax called 'chevage,' which took the form of either a lump sum down or an annual payment, had to be provided. It was this right to keep the man in the manor, combined with the right to his labour, that made him a serf, and the manor, even if it were a home for the bondsman, was in some sense also a prison. Moreover, the lord had control over the peasantry and their sons and daughters in other ways ; for example, before the marriage of a daughter, and some-

*Serfdom and the restrictions which accompanied it.*

times before that of a son, the lord's consent had to
be obtained and a fine called 'merchet' paid. In
various manors there were other claims, as, for example,
a sum might have to be paid on the lord giving per-
mission for a son to be educated for the Church, or
a fine rendered on the sale of an ox, a calf, or a nag,
or on a peasant entering into the land of his predecessor,
whilst on the death of a peasant, in some places,
the best beast on the land was claimed under the
title of a 'heriot.' Again, in some manors the lords
seem to have secured the right of wardship, which gave
them the control of land during the minority of a peasant
owner. All these claims, taken together, amounted in
many villages to a considerable burden. But in others,
especially those under the king or under the Church,
the burdens would be light and life would be freer
in its character.

Ultimately, as generations passed, the various
arrangements between the lord and the peasants, both
freemen and bondsmen, were modified; the so-called
'customs' or rules of the manor changing from time to
time as conditions changed. Payments in kind were in
many manors altered to money payments, and the
claims on the man's labour became less of a personal
character—it was sufficient for the peasant to provide a
labourer, and not necessary for him to work himself.
Concurrently, labour services tended in many manors
to be converted into money rents. As these ties were
weakened, the bondsmen became freer. But at times,
when there was a shortage of labour, the bailiffs were
inclined to go back to the old customs and demand
forced labour: and so in most manors a long struggle
went on, lasting with intervals of peace from one
generation to another, until at last, as will be seen

later, serfdom and forced labour disappeared and irritating conditions were done away with. As these changes came about the manor lost its position as a controlling element in English rural life, and the village life readjusted itself to new conditions.

# CHAPTER IV

## THE GROWTH OF FREEDOM

THE XIVth century was a period of much disorder and of rapid change. From its commencement men's minds seem to have been touched by a strong desire for freedom. Moreover, as the years passed, new ideas and new conditions of life spread through the villages as an outcome of the great historic events that marked the progress of the century.

The great national events : (1) wars, (2) plagues, and (3) agitations.

These events were four: (1) the wars; (2) the plagues; (3) the religious and social reform agitations; and (4) the Peasant Revolt of 1381. Of these the first three, belonging as they do to the national life that lay outside the village boundaries, will be dealt with separately and at once.

During almost the whole of this century England was at war, first with Scotland and later with France. Many villagers must have been drawn away to fight in these wars, and this could not fail to cause want of labour, both on the peasants' fields and on the lord's land. At the same time money was needed for the expenses of war, and heavy taxation was imposed. Much of this taxation would fall directly on the lords of the manors, who would have in their turn to extract it from the peasantry, and there must have been constant negotiations in reference to this question

5

between the lord's bailiff on the one side and the village community on the other. As an outcome of such negotiations, in return either for cash down, urgently needed for war expenses, or for settled annual payments, arrangements were made for freeing the peasants from obligations, whether week-work, or boon-work, or fines paid on the sale of stock, on marriage of daughters or on leaving a manor. With the wars, unsuccessful as they were, came also dissatisfaction and general disorder throughout the kingdom, with a gradual weakening of the discipline on which the manor depended.

Several very serious epidemics spread throughout the country in the XIVth century, but by far the worst was the Black Death, which attacked Britain in the years 1348–1350. Coming from Asia, it swept across Europe from east to west, devastating the countries through which it passed. Crossing the Channel, it spread throughout England. Perhaps half the people died. When the plague had passed away, a new problem had arisen. Instead of men wanting work, everywhere there was work wanting men, and land wanting labour.

In the history of the religious and social reform agitations, which took place in the latter half of the century, two persons stand out as conspicuous figures— Wycliffe and John Ball : the former stood for religious, the latter for personal and economic freedom. Not very much is known about either of them. Wycliffe, who lived from about 1325 to 1384, was probably first a Fellow and later Master of Balliol College, Oxford. He was a man of considerable personal charm, of independent views and of strength of character, who attained great prominence in both the religious and

political life of the time.  He vigorously attacked the
extravagance of the prelates and aristocratic rectors,
and urged that the Church should surrender its wealth
and temporal authority.  At the same time he maintained that power and dominion in spiritual matters
rested with God alone, and that everyone had within
himself the spiritual inspiration necessary for his
guidance.  In the latter years of his life, just before and
after the Peasant Revolt, he spread his views by his
books, speeches and pamphlets, whilst an order of
poor preachers, 'simple priests' as they were called,
went through the towns and villages, preaching his
gospel of spiritual freedom ; they based their teaching
directly on the Bible, which Wycliffe himself translated
into English.  His followers were called Lollards, or
babblers, and towards the end of the century they
abounded everywhere.  Unlike Wycliffe, John Ball
seems to have been of the people, and to have addressed
himself in the main to social problems.  He was a
priest, who, during the years that intervened between
the Black Death and the Peasant Revolt, spent much
of his time wandering through the South of England,
preaching in churchyards and by roadsides the
doctrines that five hundred years later were revived
under the title of Christian Socialism.  The pith of his
teaching is comprised in an oft-quoted sentence, " They
(the lords) have pleasure and fine houses : we (the
peasants) have pain and labour, the wind and the rain
in the fields : and yet it is of us and our toil that
these men hold their state."  He taught, in fact, that
the fruits of labour belonged to the labourer, and looked
to the blotting out of the manorial lords, and the
lawyers and other classes who depended upon them.
His views were certainly out of favour with the authori-

ties, for he was three times imprisoned by the Archbishop of Canterbury for his indiscreet utterances, and at least once excommunicated ; after the failure of the Peasant Revolt he was hanged, drawn and quartered.

In this time, when few could read, ideas were largely spread by the repetition of ballads, rhymes and pithy sayings. It was this custom that gave influence to William Langland, whose poetic writings show wide sympathies and great imaginative power and understanding of human life as he saw it. Langland, who seems to have been a Shropshire man, held a subsidiary position in the Church, making his living, apparently, by singing psalms for the souls of men. His best known work, describing a vision relating to Piers the Plowman, written about 1362, includes many wonderful pictures of the life of his time. Incidentally, Langland proffers much advice to members of the various classes of society with whom the poem deals. Addressing "labourers landless, that live by their hands," the men who " must highly be hired, or else he will chide," he advises them to make the most of their present advantage, which he realized would not be permanent :—

> " I warn you, ye workmen, to win while ye may ;
> For Hunger now hitherward hastens full fast."

To the manorial lord or knight he asks for justice for his tenant :—

> " O'ertax thou no tenant, save Truth will assent !
> And though thou amerce them let mercy be taxer !"

And later, in the same strain, he writes :—

> " Beguile not thy bondman, the better thou'lt speed ;
> Though under thee here, it may happen in heaven
> His seat may be higher, in saintlier bliss."

Langland's political economy differed from that of John

time private savings and property vested in the parish or any village gilds that there might be, would, when shared amongst a reduced population, tend to bring to the individuals who had survived the plague an increase of wealth. The villagers who were left alive were doubtless in a better position after the Black Death than they had been before. The lord of the manor on the other hand was in a very difficult position. He depended on the labour of the peasants, whether forced or paid for, and on their rents or services. Many of the peasants were dead, and the land of the dead, and such of the stock as had been leased with it, were, unless there were heirs to take it over, upon the lord's hands. Many of the free labourers upon whom he might have relied to cultivate his land were also dead. The lords of the manors had therefore much land on their hands and few to cultivate it, whilst their flocks and herds were in some cases wandering untended over the estate.

Bailiffs were puzzled to find either labourers to work or tenants to take land. It was not easy to find a solution. The lords let some of the arable land to the more enterprising peasants, who must have been glad to increase their holdings, especially when they could get land on good terms : later on, when affairs settled down and times improved, these men must have obtained the reward of their enterprise and become comparatively wealthy : there were many such wealthy peasant families in the next century. In other cases the lords of the manors took up sheep farming, and so avoided to a large extent the labour difficulty. But these remedies, not being generally applied, only solved the problem in a few places, while the want of labour was widespread. Consequently, wages went up rapidly.

At the same time, the peasants took advantage of the general dislocation of affairs to evade the rule of astriction which bound them to their manors ; and, leaving their villages, wandered through the land seeking for employers in town or country who would pay higher wages, or lords of the manors who would let them land at a low rent. Such employers they found, especially amongst city men of wealth, many of whom had taken advantage of the position of the lords of the manors to buy up estates.

The difficulties were, it will be seen, acute, and had to be dealt with ; so the lords devised what they thought would be a remedy. They decided to force men to work at the old wages, and with this object secured the issue of a royal ordinance and the passing of a series of Acts of Parliament,[1] known as The Statutes of Labourers. " Many," we are told, " seeing the necessity of the masters and a great scarcity of servants," will not serve unless they receive excessive wages ; so it was decreed that every unemployed man or woman under sixty, not having land or property, was bound to serve the lord or other employer who required him or her to work, and to take only the wages which were customary before the plague began. The men were to appear in the market-places, tools in hand, and undertake the work offered. The old rule whereby the tenants were attached to their manors was re-enforced by statute, and those who wandered about the country were to be treated as fugitives from justice and subjected to imprisonment and branding. This is the general outline of this series of statutes ; and although the laws were often evaded, they definitely set the men against the lords and were one of the causes

[1] See Appendix, p. 167.

of the struggle which lasted to the close of the century. At the same time such of the farming peasantry as remained working on their land were being harassed in other ways. Although the details of the questions at issue between manorial lords and their tenants are not very definitely understood, there were certain questions well suited to cause controversy. It was clearly to the lords' advantage to enforce, whenever possible, the old custom of work on the land instead of money rents, and thus secure the labour that was needed. Such a demand for forced labour, when made, would have been a fruitful source of quarrel, for the peasant farmers throughout the country must have known that in many districts their fellows had obtained their freedom from their obligations, and must have been stirred by the knowledge to secure such freedom for themselves. Moreover, there was another grievance; such of the larger farmers as needed labour could not in practice have got the benefit of the Statutes of Labourers, which were so framed as to give the lords the first claim on the labour of the unemployed. Finally, the two classes, the labourers and the peasant farmers, both of whom appear at this time to have improved their position and become better off than they had been in the earlier centuries, made common cause against the manorial lords; and for thirty years or so following the Black Death there were riots, strikes and other disorders, amounting almost to a class war.

This thirty years' controversy, which culminated in the revolt of 1381, has many interesting features. Men like the English peasants of that time, whether farmers or labourers, belonging as they did to a class that had co-operated in their work and their pleasure from the earliest times, would have had little difficulty in organizing themselves for the purposes of this struggle.

**The thirty years' struggle.** Nothing definite is known of their organization, though there are occasional references in contemporary records to a 'Great Society.' Possibly the organization of the craft gilds may have been utilized ; undoubtedly the village artisans or craftsmen, such as the millers, tilers and carters, most of whom would have been gildsmen, took a leading part in the rising of 1381. In any case, in those days it would be easy to find in a village men with special capacity for organization. Such men would come quickly to the front. It is, indeed, not too much to assume that, in the years that preceded the revolt of 1381, there was someone in most villages in the South and East of England who corresponded to the trade union secretary of the somewhat similar movement which took place under Joseph Arch, five centuries later. There were, at that time, plenty of inspiring ideas outside the general struggle for better conditions of life. The ideal of a free community without riches or poverty, was at the back of John Ball's preaching, and many songs and sayings passed from mouth to mouth emphasizing the same point of view. The English translation of the Bible perhaps also gave new thoughts to the people illustrative of this teaching.

In the middle of this turmoil and disorder a new blow was struck at the peasants. In the winter of 1380–81 the government, who were in great want of money, decided to levy a poll tax of a shilling a head on the whole population over fifteen, beggars only being excepted. This tax hit the village people especially hard through its method of collection.

Every township or vill had to provide a definite sum calculated at the rate of 1s. a head on the taxable population, but between the various inhabitants of the district the tax was graded in amount according to the wealth and position of the taxpayer ; no one, however, paying for himself and wife more than a pound or less than a groat.  In a poor township or vill every man or woman over fifteen had therefore to find a shilling, since there would be no rich to bear the brunt of the taxation by larger contributions.  This must have struck the people as extremely unfair.  The villagers found their way out of the difficulty and seemed, as a rule, to have persuaded the village constables—the officials who had charge over the collection —to send in false returns of the number of inhabitants. This practice was so widespread that the returns for many counties showed a remarkably small number of adults subject to taxation.  The government soon realized what had happened, and in the month of March a fresh levy was made.

This sordid quarrel about the taxation, coming on the top of all the other wrangles, brought matters to a head, and in the late spring of 1381 the **The Peasant Revolt.** men of the villages revolted.  Putting aside their work, they deserted their little farm-houses and cottages, and leaving their wives and children to labour, came drifting up the lanes, joining with others until their numbers mounted up to hundreds and to thousands.  And as they came they must have talked of the troubles of the past and of the days that were coming, when the old common life would be revived and there would be no lords or bailiffs to make claims on their labour, and all would live happily.

Although there were scattered risings in a large number of counties, the main revolt of the country people took place in Kent, Essex, Norfolk, Suffolk and Cambridgeshire, in which counties the movement was widespread and well organized. At first the rising appears to have been free from any great excesses, the peasants themselves must have been of a naturally orderly character ; but the discontented and degraded people of the nation appear to have collected around the peasant bands, therefore it is not surprising that before the revolt was over there was much sacking and burning of houses and killing of innocent men.

In the early days of the revolt the men of Kent, led by Wat Tyler of Essex and John Hales of Malling, took the lead. They promptly occupied Canterbury, liberated John Ball, who was in the archbishop's prison, and then marched on London. Such lawyers as they caught on their way were put to death, stewards' houses were burnt and the manorial records of their hated obligations were destroyed. The men reached London and entered the city without opposition. Indeed the city craftsmen and some, at least, of the leading citizens seem to have been on their side. Meanwhile the Essex men had concentrated at Mile End, and the Hertfordshire men, under William Grindecobbe, at Highbury and St. Albans. London was substantially in the hands of the peasant forces. The boy king, Richard II, who had already attempted to address the Kentish contingent from a boat on the river, proceeded on a Friday in June to Mile End, where he made to a large assembly consisting mostly of Essex men, certain definite promises. Serfdom would be abolished, services and obligations set aside and all holders of land were apparently to become free tenants paying a fixed annual rent to their manorial lord. Subsequently he issued charters bestowing freedom and amnesty, and presented banners to the leaders as a token of his approval. His promises, circulated throughout the peasant forces, sent many home happy and satisfied. They were, they thought, to be free men, and to have permanent tenancies at a fixed rent. However, the more disorderly section of the people remained in London, and the sacking of houses and the killing of innocent people went on all that day and night. On the following day Wat Tyler was killed, on the occasion of an interview with the king at Smithfield where he had submitted fresh demands, and the crowd was dispersed by a contingent of the king's soldiers.

The rising, so far as it centred in London, was now practically over and the peasants were hurrying back to their homes, when the young king, acting doubtless on his ministers' advice, repudiated his promises of freedom and sent out men-at-arms on a mission of repression throughout the country. The peasants showed little fight, though one strong contingent collected at the edge of the woods at Billericay in Essex; they were, it seems, completely beaten, and are said to have lost 500 men. Events somewhat similar to those that took place in and around London, occurred throughout East Anglia, and where risings took place promises were given and many charters were issued. But in no cases were the promises acted upon. The policy of repression was adopted everywhere, and those of the peasants who showed fight were overwhelmed by the better armed forces of the king or his retainers, or of the local nobles or bishops who organized forces for the suppression of the risings.

Parliament, convened in the following winter, supported the royal repudiation : the bondsmen were, in the view of this authority, the 'goods of the lords of the manors,' and such they must remain. But, in coming to this decision, judgment was tempered with mercy, for with some exceptions it was decided to grant an amnesty to those who had taken part in the movement.

The Peasant Revolt was a remarkable movement; never before or since has the English peasantry combined on so large a scale or been so well and successfully led. They were defeated by a political ruse—promises of freedom and reform, only made to be repudiated at the first convenient moment. The results were therefore slight in proportion to the character of the rising.

It is true that personal freedom was ultimately attained, but the change came slowly ; indeed, serfdom continued in many villages until the reign of Elizabeth, and occasionally to a far later date. Another of the peasants' proposals, the appropriation of Church land, was not dealt with for many generations, whilst the peasants failed to secure what was perhaps their most important object, the general commutation of services and the institution of permanent tenancies at a fixed rent. Had the peasants succeeded throughout England as a whole in obtaining this particular demand, permanency of tenure would have been secured. As a result, the loss of land that accompanied enclosures in the following centuries could hardly have occurred, and the creation of a mass of destitute and landless people might have been avoided.

Results of the revolt.

Peasant life of the old style, already beginning to decay in the XIVth century, had its peculiar features of which it is desirable to obtain some general impression, before proceeding to consider the reconstruction of rural England that began in the later years of that century.

Mediaeval village life.

The peasantry, who formed the bulk of the nation, lived a hard life and were occasionally the victims of great disasters, famines, plagues and devastating armies. But there is little reason to believe that the life was degraded: the peasants, indeed, lived in close touch with nature, and from nature they derived not only a certain breadth of vision but a definite religious outlook on life. This outlook accorded with the position held in those days by the Church, a body powerful not only in spiritual but in material matters. In the village the Church was represented by the priest, a man who had much work to do outside his religious duties. Not only had he land to cultivate, but much public business fell to him. He took a leading part in the parish meetings and other forms of local government, worked with his parishioners in the gilds, if such there were, and in the organization of amusements and social life; relieved poverty with a share of the tithes or other dues that came into his hands, and generally kept in close touch with the peoples' lives. Sometimes he himself belonged to the peasant class, and in few cases could he have been much above it, for the aristocratic rector, though not unknown, must have been a rarity. The Church was also represented by the great monasteries and the prelates, controlling as landholders a large part of the countryside: they had a widespread influence even beyond their own estates, through the help they gave in the relief of sickness and of poverty, and their power to protect the people from oppression.

The villager had much social life and many duties outside the cultivation of the land. As a member of the village gild he would have a part to play in helping the priest in his care of the poor and sick ; he helped, with funds, members on pilgrimage and welcomed them on their return, and when death came to any member, he provided prayers for the soul. The gilds would arrange a religious and social meeting on the day of the patron saint of the village church, to which all the population would come ; and might also organize plays and pageants. The peasant had too his public duties, his village meetings and the courts of the manor to attend, and he might be called to local hundred and other courts. He had also to see that the customs of the manor were enforced and the land kept in cultivation. He would probably at some time in his life have to act as a reeve, or a constable, or as a foreman of the fields or other official, and at any time he might be called off from work on his own or the lord's land to repair bridges or fortresses, or perhaps to fight for his lord, either in some petty quarrel or in the nation's wars.

Although the rule of astriction tied men to the manors, most of the young men of the peasant class must have made an opportunity to leave their homes in search of adventure. Many evaded lord and bailiff and slipped away without leave, others left their homes on military duties or on a pilgrimage by leave of the Church. Men who had once got beyond the manor boundary must have wandered as fancy took them from place to place, meeting many strange travellers on the strips of rough grass land that at that time served as roads. The king himself was constantly moving about with his retainers, in order to visit and draw supplies of provisions and tribute from various parts of the country. Abbots, bishops and nobles journeyed from manor to manor, and such great men must have had numerous followers. Pedlars, musicians and beggars tramped from fair to fair, taking markets, perhaps, on their route: hermits were settled in way-side huts, and not only priests but robed monks and friars were to be met with on the road.

For those countrymen who had no love of adventure and did not wish to go far afield there were—at least—markets and fairs to attend. The villages were largely self-supporting, and there was no great amount of national trade such as we have to-day; but market centres were numerous, and many great and important fairs were held annually throughout England under the protection of the king, of the Church or of some great layman owning trading rights. Market day was an occasion for social meeting even in the XIVth century, and all the village must have gone to the fairs.

It will thus be realized that whilst the life differed greatly from the life of to-day, it must have been full of interest; it obtained too a special character owing to the democratic and co-operative spirit that prevailed amongst the people, and influenced not only their work on the land but also their social life and public duties.

# PART II

(About 1381–1820)

## THE RECONSTRUCTION OF RURAL LIFE

### CHAPTER V

#### CIVILIZATION AND ITS EFFECT ON RURAL LIFE

In the Middle Ages statesmen looked to the land for the provision of food for the nation and for the breeding of a race of men able to fight for their lords and for the king. But from the XVth century the breeding of men became, by degrees, a secondary matter, for there was less and less fighting for the peasantry to do. And at the same time money and the accumulation of wealth began more and more to influence men's minds. As a result, a large part of the life of the country-side, like the life of the rest of England, has been gradually reconstructed on a commercial basis. Modern civilization has come to us through the channels of commerce.

*The intrusion of commerce.*

Broadly speaking, the changes in rural life that have so come are these. In the first place, the restrictions affecting the lives and the work of the peasantry continued to disappear; and by degrees the bondsmen attained complete personal freedom.

*Personal freedom.*

66

The peasant farmers so freed lost ground in another direction : they lost their hold on the land. The old manorial tenant, the bondsman, although he had no legal rights enforceable in the national courts, had nevertheless a real grip on the soil ; but during the period of reconstruction the copyholders and other customary tenants were largely squeezed out, to be replaced by farmers who took land on annual tenancies or on leases for lives or for years, holding on a less continuous tenure than the old peasant families.

Tenants by custom replaced by leaseholders.

Concurrently, the number of hired labourers, a very small body in early days, increased considerably, and from the XIVth century onward the agricultural labourer has formed a definite class in rural life.

Landless labourers.

Another change of great importance came about on the appropriation and re-arrangement of land through what are called enclosures. As used in rural history, the word 'enclosure' indicates the enclosing of the land within new boundaries, when any part of an estate is converted from property subject to common control or common use to private ownership : it contains the two ideas : the fencing in of the land and the withdrawing of it from a common use. Enclosures are responsible for the dividing up of the land into fenced fields, parks and woods, such as we see to-day. Enclosure has been going on since the earliest times, and is still occurring in a few places. In the XIVth century it certainly became a common practice. These enclosures have been carried out in many ways and have had many different

Enclosures—

results ; but whatever the process employed, the rights of future generations have been, with rare exceptions, ignored. In old days, children born into a village community had prospective rights in the arable and the commons, and were in that sense property owners : but after enclosure, such children had lost such prospects, they started life lower on the social ladder.

Whilst enclosures impoverished a class in one direction, they appear to have enriched England in another. Especially was this so in the XVIIIth century, when the 'new agriculture' accompanied the enclosures. With it came improved cattle, sheep and other live stock, greatly increased crops of corn, widespread use of turnips and other roots and of clover and similar grasses, the development of labour-saving machinery and, as a result, a remarkable increase in the productivity of the land. The outcome was not, as in some other countries, market gardening and small holding by little men, but farming by big farmers holding from hundreds to thousands of acres of land.

*—and the 'new agriculture.'*

The position of the Church and its relation to country life also altered in these centuries. In the XVth century many prelates and parsons were carried away by the new commercial spirit, and some even took an active part in commerce. There was much extravagance and some arrogance and neglect of spiritual duties. The estrangement between the Church and the people thus created made it possible for Henry VIII and Edward VI to appropriate, without a national protest, much of its wealth. The Church then ceased to be the

**The Church.**

greatest landowner of the country and was replaced by numerous private holders. At the same time this loss of wealth compelled it to relinquish much of its work of relief of poverty ; this responsibility for the poor was in part taken up by private individuals and by voluntary associations such as the gilds : whilst later, when the voluntary method failed, the legislature intervened to create the 'poor law,' which put the responsibility on the nation. Meanwhile another change—in the direction of independence of thought—took place in the religious life, culminating in the movement with which the Puritans were associated in the XVIIth century. This was followed by the foundation of the Nonconformist movement, which stood outside the Anglican Church, and from that time onward the villages of England have been divided into two religious camps.

Concurrently with these changes came alterations in government. From the XIVth century onwards that section of the upper classes which consisted

Local and central government.

of the old landholding families, recruited by the town merchants and lawyers, have had a growing influence in English public life. After the fall of the Stuarts, this influence increased and this section of society was able to gather into its own hands the administration of Parliament, of rural local government, administered in quarter and petty sessions, and of rural justice.

The new forms that government took were accompanied by new work and responsibilities, and at the same time methods of taxation and rating were revised and put on the basis that prevails to-day.

Although the county gentry in their sessions controlled the general administration of county affairs,

the village communities, gathered together under the
title of the parish, maintained their position, and were,
in the XVIth century, given a clear status when they
were made definitely responsible both for the roads
and for the administration of the poor law. These
two questions assumed an increasing importance as
time went on, and gave the parish officials much work
to do, until their transference to new authorities in
the XIXth century.

The decay both of the manorial system and the
feudal organization that stood above it, and the introduction of the commercial point of view,
New people developed a new style of countryman, who
and new
features. very gradually replaced the old type. The
lord, the governor of the manor, was replaced by the squire, the peasant gave way to the
farmer, and the village craftsman lost ground through
the competition of the artisans and shopkeepers of
the country towns: dealers obtained an increased
importance, and where they aided their business by
money-lending, became a strong influence in country
life: whilst, of course, the labouring class grew. At
the same time England ceased to be primarily an
agricultural country, and trade and manufacture
became the main national interest.

Two incidents that occurred in Tudor times—
the breakdown of the system of entails and the dissolution of the monasteries—brought, for the first time in
English history, a very large amount of land into the
market, and although the old system of vesting land in
families was practically reconstructed by the lawyers,
two hundred years later, by their ingenious system of
land settlements, buying and selling of land became and

game provided valuable winter food. A statute[1] was also enacted directed to keeping the country people in the country, by forbidding the apprenticeship of country children to trades in the town ; and, about the same time, the Universities closed their doors to the peasants' children, and so probably put an end to the peasant priests, a class that seems in earlier days to have taken the side of the people in their controversies with the manorial lords. Nevertheless, on the whole the peasants steadily if slowly improved their position. Undoubtedly the more intelligent of the lords of the manors, who must have seen that it profited them little to spend their lives quarrelling with the tenants, continued to commute the old obligations and services for money rents, and to deal with their estates by the new methods. Some took up sheep farming ; others let off the home farm. Some let off the whole manor : and we know that in certain manors such leases were granted to the bailiffs or to the village community as a whole. By the close of the XIVth century the struggle was dying out, and a new generation had arisen, imbued with new ideas.

The period which began with the new century divides itself naturally into two parts, the first extending up to about 1485, the beginning of the Tudor period, and the second continuing from that time until the middle of the XVIIth century.

Prosperity and disorder in the XVth century.

The XVth century appears to have been, on the whole, a prosperous time for country people ; yet there were certain strong cross currents of events that seem inconsistent with this general condition. Un-

[1] See Appendix, p. 167.

doubtedly it was a time of much disorder, whilst in
addition there were many plagues, more virulent certainly in the town than the country, and also several
years of famine, which may have been local rather than
national. It is difficult to reconcile these apparent
inconsistencies : the fact seems to be that the nation,
owing to the spread of trade, was getting rapidly richer,
and the country people, as a whole, benefited accordingly. But at the same time this growth of prosperity
was checked by the disorders. These disorders were
widespread : it was not only that the Wars of the
Roses went on intermittently, but many of the great
nobles and large landowners carried on their private
quarrels by force of arms. The lawlessness of the
period had one interesting indirect effect: it gave a
special opening to those of the young men of the
villages who wished to free themselves from bondage
and secure an adventurous life. Such men, like the
' commended ' men of the XIth century, attached themselves to a superior, and taking the ' livery ' of some
great baron, some abbot or knight, secured ' maintenance.' They were then of the retinue of their new
lord and were responsible to him alone ; in return they
fought for him in case of need. When, later on, these
retinues were broken up by the Tudors, a large number
of these men lost their employment and were thrust
down into the poverty-stricken class.

The peasants also fought in their own quarrels. The
Lollards appear to have fanned the flame which caused
turmoils early in the century, and there was in 1431 a
mob of peasants who combined under the leadership of
a certain Jack Straw but the principal peasant rising of
the XVth century took place under Jack Cade in 1450.
In this year the Kentish men, who were Cade's principal

supporters, came together in force, under the headmen of their hundreds, to support this wild Irishman, who to the peasants was 'John Amendall.' Cade's men gathered in the first instance at Blackheath, but withdrew to Sevenoaks, where they defeated a royal force sent after them. Later they returned to the neighbourhood of London, camping at Southwark, on the south side of the river. Cade, who assumed the name of 'Mortimer,' rode unmolested through London and proclaimed himself 'Lord of the City'; but a few days after this adventure he was beaten in a battle on London Bridge. His followers, to whom pardon was promised, scattered to their homes, but Cade himself was caught and executed.

People, it is important to note, quarrelled not only in the counties, but in the law courts, by that time constructed on the modern basis, and as a result many lawyers, a new class created to plead in the new courts, became rich.

It was in this century that the development of enclosures—the cutting of pieces of land out of the manorial estate, fencing them in and con-

**Enclosures.** verting them to private use—went on on such a scale as to be considered for the first time a very serious matter. It will be clearly understood that most estates were, at the beginning of this period, still cultivated on the communal lines already described; peasants had, as a rule, their small strips of land scattered over the open arable fields, their plots in the meadowland, and their common rights of pasturage and rights to wood for fuel and other purposes, over the commons, woods and wastes.

How, then, were these rights destroyed and the estates enclosed? Enclosures were carried out in this period (1) by definite agreement, (2) by gradual adjustment and (3) by appropriation.

Enclosures by agreement occurred occasionally, when the tenants and the lord of a manor came to a definite arrangement for redividing and fencing in the land. Under such an arrangement, the peasant owners of the scattered strips gave up their holdings in order to obtain a block of arable land, the open arable fields being, for this purpose, rearranged and each man's strips thrown together. The blocks of land so created were fenced in and became the holding of the tenant, replacing his many scattered strips. Such a process is going on to-day at Laxton. Some portion of the commons, woods and wastes might also be divided up, allotted to the tenants of the arable and by them formed into fields for pasture or even ploughed up for corn : whilst the lord of the manor might obtain similar holdings on a larger scale. Thus, perhaps in a single year, the open arable fields with their many strips, the meadows and a large part of the commons, woods and wastes might disappear, to be replaced by fenced-in fields.

Enclosure by adjustment—a more gradual process— was probably more usual than enclosure by definite agreement. The tenants of the manor would in this case exchange a strip here and a strip there, until by degrees, in perhaps a couple of generations, the greater part of the open arable fields and meadows would have been rearranged into blocks, which the tenants would, from time to time, fence in. In the same way, portions of the commons might be enclosed, or colonized by the tenants, without perhaps any formal agreement ; one tenant taking a piece here, perhaps only a site for a squatter's cottage, another land there, and the lord also taking an area in to compensate him for his loss of common rights.

Both of these forms of enclosure produced finally the same results, and when carried out fairly, were of benefit to those immediately concerned. The old manorial estate continued in a modified form and the general character of the life was preserved. There still remained in the village a large number of small holders with many common interests, but they could grow more corn on their enclosed blocks of arable, and their sheep and stock would do better on the enclosed pasture.

These two methods of enclosure, which had been going on on a small scale since very early days, were largely employed in the XVth century, so that, before the end of that century, almost all of Kent, Essex, Suffolk, Devonshire and Cornwall were enclosed,[1] and in the main in the occupation of small proprietors.

Enclosure by appropriation, the third method, was something entirely different. It consisted in the appropriation of the common pastures, woods and wastes, and sometimes even the open arable fields and meadows, and the very cottages of the peasants by the lords of the manors or by other large holders of estates. As a rule, in the XVth century, such appropriations were only carried out on a moderate scale and were justified in law by the Statutes of Merton and Westminster.[2] If they extended only to the taking in of a small part out of a large area of common land, woods or wastes, such enclosures would have little effect, for the village

[1] It is suggested by some authorities that the open field system never prevailed in parts of these counties.
[2] See Appendix, p. 168.

might still have ample common land for the feeding of the peasants' stock. But if these encroachments and enclosures went on year by year, and the commons, woods and wastes were greatly reduced, it might mean ruin for the small peasant holder, whose system of farming was such that, without his stock and his pasture for stock, he would be beaten in his struggle for existence. He was even in worse plight when, as sometimes occurred, a lord of the manor proceeded with one of the great enclosures that swept away the whole of the peasants' property, destroying even the villages, and turning a large part, and sometimes the whole, of the manorial estate into one great sheep farm. Such great enclosures had begun in the XVth century, before the reign of Henry VII, but it was not until the XVIth century that they became so widespread as to threaten a national disaster.

Enclosure of the second type, by gradual adjustment, was the characteristic method of the XVth century.

Following enclosure by agreement or adjustment, a system of cultivation called 'convertible farming' was adopted in some counties. Under this **Convertible farming.** method, the farmer's holding was divided into six fields. Of these, three were set aside for corn and farmed on the three-course system— winter corn, spring corn and fallow ; of the other three, one each year was allotted to the cows, another to sheep and perhaps other stock, and the third set aside for hay. After a certain number of years, there was an interchange, and the arable fields were allowed to go down to grass and the grass fields were ploughed up. This method of cultivation, which has features in common with the modern mixed farm, employed a greater number of men than sheep farming, and also gave men work in hedging and ditching.

During the XVth century the manufacture of cloth in home industries and small factories spread throughout England, until, by the middle of the century, it was said in Parliament that the making of cloth was 'the greatest living and occupation of poor people.' The weaving shops, carried on largely in conjunction with small farming, were widespread in the villages of Norfolk, Suffolk, Essex, Kent and Cambridge, in the east; in Westmorland, Lancashire and Yorkshire in the north; in Sussex, Hampshire, Devonshire, Dorset and Cornwall in the south, and also in some of the Midland Counties. The cloth so made was eagerly bought up for export, as English cloth had already attained a European reputation. This growth of weaving and the home industry of spinning that accompanied it, went hand in hand with an increase in the flocks of sheep. This increase greatly impressed writers of the time, who constantly refer to the enormous number of sheep to be seen in England. Sheep farming for the sale of wool was undoubtedly profitable, and all classes on the land benefited. It does not follow that arable farming was unprofitable. The government being, as a rule, sympathetic to the cultivators and anxious to encourage arable farming, legislation was directed towards keeping corn at a fair price.[1] Exportation of wheat was allowed only when the price fell below 6s. 8d. a quarter, and importation was not permitted unless it was above that figure. This tended to keep the price uniform. Similar

*Growth of wool trade and agriculture.*

---

[1] See Appendix, p. 172.

legislation was passed with the object of securing a
steady price for barley and rye of 3s. and 4s. a quarter
respectively.   Uniformity of price has always been
beneficial to agriculture, since it eliminates the element
of speculation.   Hop growing also extended in this
century, since the brewing of beer from malt and hops
then introduced, was beginning to oust the Anglo-Saxon
ale made of malt only.

With this prosperity and the weakening of the
manorial system, came the occasional taking over by
the more prosperous peasants of the land
**Prosperity** of their less successful neighbours.  As a
**and the**
**social life.** result, towards the end of the century,
instead of the typical old-fashioned village
community, consisting of two groups of peasants, one
holding perhaps, as a rule, thirty strips of land and
the other five, there were to be found not only a class
of landless men (who were doing well, for wages were
going up rapidly), but also men with holdings of all
sizes, from an acre up to a hundred or even more.
Thus was created a ladder up which men might climb.
Many of the peasants benefited by this change, and
some may have become freeholders ; but the bulk of
these successful men must have been holders of land
on the old manorial terms, copyholders as a rule,
paying a customary rent, well below the real value
of the land and standing together to maintain the
customs of their particular manor.   Without being
very far from the truth, these peasant farmers may
be pictured as a burly, turbulent, good-natured, jovial
class, fighting for their old customs and using what remained of the old manorial system as a bulwark against
the encroachments of the lord and the large farmers.

In addition to these customary tenants, other classes were at that time rapidly increasing. On the lords' land were the large farmers, freeholders or leaseholders, men of substance, with great flocks of sheep, good houses, and plenty of money in their pockets. And again, in many villages there were to be found not only spinning and weaving, but craftsmen and artisans carrying on industries, such as worsted in Norfolk and iron foundries in Surrey, Sussex, and Hampshire. As industries grew, traders came to the market towns and villages to buy wool, cloth, and iron and other materials, and cattle, pigs and fowls, corn and fruit for the London market. Such men created a new element in country life. The whole life was, indeed, at the beginning of a great change: there was more enterprise, more competition, more opportunity, and more variety. But the changes did not come everywhere; in the North of England especially, where men were wanted to fight against the Scots, the old system continued. But on the whole the growth was rapid, and would have been even more marked had there not been such sudden misfortunes as plagues, famines and destruction of crops by armies engaged in the wars or by bodies of men retained for some private quarrel. When, towards the end of the century, the wars and private quarrels had died out and internal peace was being secured under Tudor rule, it seemed as if the English peasantry were on a broad high-road towards prosperity; and that England would become a country of enterprising small holders, peasant proprietors of the type that are to be found, even at the present day, in such places as the Isle of Axholme, where the old system has developed undisturbed. But, as a fact, a different fate was in store for rural England.

7

fall daily to theft and robbery or pitifully die for hunger and cold." It appears that the flocks of individual proprietors sometimes extended to 24,000 sheep. The laws [1] passed at various times during this period directed the rebuilding of farm-houses, the return of the land to tillage, and especially ordered that no one person was to hold more than 2,000 sheep; whilst the position of the landless men was dealt with by a statute [2] of Queen Elizabeth's reign which ordered that no cottage was to be built unless provided with at least four acres of land. These laws were constantly evaded: indeed, for generations there was no one to enforce them except the justices of the peace, themselves perhaps offenders. Flocks were divided by the holders amongst their families and servants, apportioning 2,000 to each, a single room in a ruined farm-house was repaired, a single furrow run across the sheep-walks. By such means the law was easily evaded. But the government did not accept these evasions without a struggle: the law courts, inspired by the Council of State, undertook to protect the tenants, wherever possible, by giving the force of law to the customs of a manor, while the government on various occasions appointed commissioners [3] both to make inquiries and to see that the law was enforced.

In some cases the peasants succumbed to the arbitrary encroachments on their rights, and wandered off to other manors; in other cases, they bargained for terms and got some compensation when appropriations took place; but many independent men who were not inclined to give way decided not to trouble law courts or government,

*The peasants' action.*

[1] See Appendix, pp. 169, 170.   [2] Ibid. p. 174.   [3] Ibid. p. 170.

but to fight the question out in their own way. Some assembled in bands, armed themselves and drove off the enclosers, whilst others took part in the local risings that occurred from time to time between 1530 and 1560. Of these, the most remarkable was that which took place in Norfolk in 1549, when Robert Ket, lord of the manor of Wymondham, and his brother William gathered 16,000 men into a camp outside Norwich. He captured, and for a little while dominated the city, whilst his men caught and hanged on the 'Reformers' Tree' near Wymondham landlords whom they deemed guilty of unjust enclosure. Apart from this extremely arbitrary action, the rising seems to have been orderly and directed towards obtaining definite reforms, not dissimilar from those demanded by Tyler in the XIVth century. Ket asked first for fixed rents, and a small fine only on transfer of land : these two reforms together would have given fixity of tenure to the peasant families—the dream of the tenants of England in all generations. Further, the peasants' common rights were not to be prejudiced by the lord stocking the commons with his beasts and sheep ; whilst rabbits, at that time considered a nuisance, were to be preserved only on land properly fenced in. Further than this Ket like Tyler protested against the holding of land by the Church and, also like Tyler, claimed freedom for all men. Moreover, the peasants asked that commissioners should be appointed to administer the law on enclosures—a course, as has been seen, subsequently adopted. The government, after some hesitation and negotiation with Ket, decided to crush the movement, and sent the Earl of Warwick to Norwich with a force which was strengthened by 1,400 German mercenaries. The peasants were easily beaten by the trained men and scattered to their homes.  The Council of State seems to have sympathized to some extent with the peasants, for the ringleaders, other than Ket, were pardoned, and Ket himself was only executed on his proudly refusing the reprieve offered him, alleging that 'just men need no pardon.'  This was the last time that the English peasantry rose in sufficient force to make an effective demonstration against the forces of the king : but local protests against enclosures continued, the most noticeable being the action of the Diggers and the Levellers during the first half of the XVIIth century.

Contemporary authorities tell a great deal of the appropriations for sheep farming and the other troubles and difficulties which continued well into the XVIIth century, but the worst evils must, in the main, have been confined to those districts where enclosures on a large scale and sheep farming marched hand in hand. Enclosures and the changes that accompanied them were certainly not universal, since, at the beginning of the XVIIIth century, it is generally supposed that more than half of the cultivated area of England was still farmed on the old system of open arable fields and commons.

Rural life was greatly affected by the suppression of the monasteries and appropriation of their manors and other land by Henry VIII ;[1] he, whilst

Suppression of monasteries.

announcing his intention of disposing of these estates "to the honour of God and the wealth of the nation," proceeded to sell or to distribute them amongst his courtiers and others, who in their turn in many cases again sold the pro-

[1] See Appendix, p. 176.

perties. One-fifteenth part of England, some authorities conjecture, so changed hands in the course of a few years ; other writers think that far more land was dealt with. Probably as many as eight thousand monks, nuns and friars were at the same time impoverished. Their dependents involved in this catastrophe may have numbered ten times as many. Eighty to ninety thousand individuals thrown, even temporarily, out of employ in the course of a few years must have caused much misery, suffering and poverty. Moreover, the disappearance of the monasteries was a blow to agriculture, for some, at least, of the monks were good farmers, collecting information both at home and abroad, and constantly making experiments with seeds introduced from other countries ; whilst their successors were, to quote Sir Thomas More, "covetous and insatiable cormorants," who knew little about agriculture. These new men looked to their land to provide them with an income : they wanted to secure money either from sheep farms or from rents. As a result, on the old monastic land, even in those places where there were no appropriations, the copyholders and other customary tenants who held at fixed and moderate rents, were often deprived of their land, and leaseholders, at higher rents, took their places.

The increase of trade and the good profits made by those farmers who could obtain land on reasonable terms resulted, notwithstanding all the troubles of the times, in the growth of wealth. The change was marked by the building of many fine churches and manor houses, replacing the older simpler buildings of a simpler time. The re-introduction of bricks

The raising of the standard of life.

and wider use of glass gave impulse to this movement. Into many of these new homes came the landlords from the towns, bringing with them new ideas of
luxury and comfort ; and round their houses beautiful
gardens were laid out, in which not only fruit and
vegetables, including potatoes and turnips, but many
flowers were grown. Doubtless many of the old lords
adopted these new ways. Improved farm-houses also
became common throughout England, brick and stone
replacing wood and wattle. Here lived the new leaseholders, the small freeholders, and the more wealthy of
the copyholding peasants. These men formed the class
of yeomen, a title given at that time to the more substantial landholders below the rank of gentlemen. In
some districts even the smaller farm-houses and cottages
appear to have improved, and both farmers and cottagers, if they had the good fortune to be outside
the area of the great enclosures, attained a higher
standard of comfort. The men's food was certainly
better. We are told by Tusser, the well-known rhym-
ing writer of that time, that—

"Good ploughmen look weekly of custom and right
For roast beef on Sundays and Thursdays at night."

There were indeed from the XVth century onward a
number of farmers and labourers and village artisans
living busy, active, successful lives in comparative comfort. There can be no doubt of this ; indeed, the widespread amusements and general gaiety that prevailed
during all this period, and especially in Elizabethan
times, show clearly that many of the villagers had
time and money to spare, and were in no sense dominated by the pressure of poverty. And yet the mass
of poverty-stricken people increased, whilst the drift

of the country people to the towns, which had begun in the XIVth century, continued.

As the general character of the country life slowly changed, approaching more and more to the type that we hear described by old villagers of to-day
**Government.** as existing in old-fashioned places up to the middle of the last century, the part taken by the people not only in central government, but in local affairs, diminished. Until the year 1430 all freeholders, however small their holding, could vote for members of Parliament, and it is possible that other persons connected with the land, even though only leaseholders or copyholders, also took part in the elections ; but in 1430[1] a law was carried through Parliament directed against voters 'whereof every of them pretend a voice equivalent with the most worthy knights and esquires dwelling within the same counties.' This act definitely limited the franchise to freeholders owning land worth 40s. a year. When it is realized that forty shillings represented about twenty-five pounds in modern money values, it will be understood that a large section of the country people were deprived of the vote. A corresponding change took place in local affairs. The decay of the common system of farming was followed by the disappearance of many of the field juries and other committees of management : at the same time, the manorial courts were losing their power, and the effective control of what manorial business remained gradually passed into the hands either of the freeholders or of the lord of the manor and his steward. Further than this, the great part of the criminal and

[1] See Appendix, p. 167.

other legal business transacted by the hundred and shire courts had, by the end of this period, passed into the hands of the justices of the peace in petty or quarter sessions, who, established towards the beginning of the XIVth century,[1] became more and more important as time went on. A further share of judicial business went to the high courts, which in this period obtained an increased importance.

The justices of the peace in quarter sessions began also to obtain definite administrative duties. In 1530[2] the care of the bridges on main roads was placed in their hands, and from that time onwards they gradually secured more and more the control of county government. On the other hand, the parish as a civil, rather than as a purely religious organization, the successor of the vill,[3] was emerging at that time from under the shadow of the decaying manor. This authority, which acted through its public assembly or vestry, as it came to be called, is found in the XVth century enjoying considerable power in the administration of parish affairs, including in some cases the management of property for the village community. Later there fell upon it the duty of repairing the roads and the responsibility of the poor, two important matters referred to below.

There seems to have been a tendency in mediaeval times to include the repair of roads in the *trinoda necessitas* and throw responsibility for it Roads. on the landholders; but this responsibility was ill-defined and, in the XVth century, when the growth of trade was followed by a demand for better roads, there arose constantly a difficulty

[1] See Appendix, p. 176.    [2] Ibid. p. 173.    [3] Ibid. p. 163.

in fixing the duty of road repairs on any particular persons. Sometimes the sheriffs seem to have taken responsibility, sometimes lords of the manor, sometimes the monasteries, sometimes private individuals. These haphazard methods did not lead to effective administration, and the old roads fell into further decay. The government at last decided to lay down some general rule. In the year 1555 [1] a statute was passed which definitely fixed the responsibility upon the parishes, subject to the supervision of the justices ; and it was further decided that the parishioners themselves were to do the necessary repairs. The leading farmers were to provide carts and horses or oxen, and the smaller holders and labourers were to give their services. The work was to be carried out under the direction of the highway overseer, an unpaid official. This system never worked well, and the condition of the roads of England remained a scandal for many generations.

From the XVth century onwards the influence of the Church on village life waned. This was due to a variety of causes. The commercial spirit **The Church, the gilds, and poverty.** seems to have been accompanied by the decadence of religion of the old type, whilst under its influence some parsons went into business or concerned themselves more with the collection of their dues than the care of their parishioners, while others held many parishes and gave attention to none. Monasteries, before their dissolution, were often centres of every sort of irregularity, and personal indulgence and extravagant habits took the place of relief of the poor and the entertaining of travellers.

[1] See Appendix, p. 173.

Moreover, in the Elizabethan age and the first half of the following century the energy of the Church was, owing to the quarrels between Presbyterians, Roman Catholics and Anglicans, diverted from good works to controversy.

In the XVth century much of the work of relieving poverty that the Church had previously undertaken had already devolved on village societies or gilds. At that time all the men of the various trades in a country district combined as a matter of course into societies or gilds of their own ; there were also many social and religious gilds, consisting not only of men, but of ' wives ' or of ' maidens.' These associations were spread throughout the country, and were influential and important in the XVth and in the first half of the XVIth centuries. They acted, it appears, as savings banks, possibly lent money to members, and by undertaking the work of sick and benefit societies gave help to the poor. The gilds also appear to have organized and paid the expenses of pageants and plays, and probably arranged the games and amusements that were characteristic of the age and gave to England its title of ' Merry England.' They kept people together and the village alive. Unfortunately, Edward VI passed a statute [1] which resulted in the appropriation of such part of the property of gilds as was employed in religious purposes, and some, though not all, of these societies must have been destroyed. It seems as if at this time the passion for appropriation of Church property spread throughout the country, and much of the miscellaneous property of the parish churches passed into lay hands. The destruction of the wealth of the Church

[1] See Appendix, p. 176.

and the decay of the gilds left the poor in a pitiable condition.

There was, of course, always a large number of poor people, and in the XVth century the pauper class probably increased when the growth of competition, which brought some men to the front, crushed others down. There were many broken men tramping the country-side after the retinues of the great nobles and ecclesiastics were disbanded in the early years of the Tudor period, and the enclosures and appropriations threw many men upon the roads. It is therefore not surprising to find that in the XVIth century the country was full of paupers and sturdy beggars. Thereupon the government took action, and legislation was constantly introduced to punish the sturdy and help the impotent. This legislation,[1] too complicated to analyse in detail, culminated in an important statute passed in 1601, the 'old poor law' of Elizabeth's reign, which laid down rules for dealing with the poor which lasted, with modifications, until the reconstruction that took place in 1834. Under the provisions of this legislation, each parish became responsible for its poor. Parish overseers were appointed by the justices annually to deal with the problem of poverty, and were empowered to levy a poor rate. Pauper children were to be apprenticed to trades, whilst able-bodied paupers were to be set to work upon the stocks of wool, hemp, etc., purchased for the purpose. Upon parents and children was thrown a responsibility to contribute towards the expenses of their poverty-stricken relations. Houses of correction were to be set up for those who refused to work, and tramps were to be whipped and sent back to their parish or their last place of 'settlement.' And

[1] See Appendix, p. 170.

so it came about that the poor villager, who in the past had relied on the casual yet kindly charity of the Church, or of individuals or gilds, was thenceforth to be treated, in common with tramps and sturdy beggars, under a severe system. From that time onward the poor, a definite and large class of rural society, were made the victims of innumerable experiments, legislative and administrative.

# CHAPTER VII

## COUNTRY LIFE IN THE TIME OF THE STUARTS

DURING the XVIIth century the life of the country continued in its gradual change from the old style to the new. On the land, the open fields culti-

**Continuation of gradual change.** vated by the peasant farmers of the old school still predominated, whilst the en-

closed fields were, as a rule, in the hands of more enterprising men, who employed capital and farmed the land on a larger scale. But the essential mediaeval features of the life had died out. Serfdom had gone : the people were free. The lord of the manor, in so far as he was a governor of his estate, also disappeared as the feudal and military conditions died out or were put an end to by legislation. He was replaced by the squire, who ruled his village, so far as he did rule it, by force of his position as justice of the peace. Moreover, the character of the landholding population was changing. A good deal of the land had, it should be observed, been bought up by farmers, and as a result it appears that in this century the peasant proprietors and other occupying owners were more numerous than they had been before or have been since. These men flourished and formed the backbone of the important 'yeoman' class. Moreover, large buyers belonging to a different class continued to come from the towns. One writer complains that land was bought up by cooks, vintners, innkeepers, dancing masters "and such trifling fellows," whilst Fynes Morison, who wrote on this subject early in the XVIIth century, speaks of the intrusion into the country of "lawyers, citizens, and vulgar men." These new men might have been 'vulgar,' but they could not fail, from their training, to be men of business ability and when they brought their capacity to bear on country problems, important new developments are seen to be beginning. In the first place the new men succeeded in reintroducing a method of keeping estates in the same family from generation to generation. The system employed was similar in effect to that existing in mediaeval times, but the method was new : great estates were not subjected to the old law of entail, but were 'settled,' as it was called. Such settlements defined how the estates were to be handed down from generation to generation amongst the descendants of the original maker of the settlement, and trustees were appointed to see that these arrangements were carried out. Settlements effectively preserved the ownership of the estates in the large landholding families, and helped both to keep the gentry at the top of the social ladder and to prevent other classes of country people from rising. They went far to preserve for the English country-side the semi-feudal character that has continued up to quite recent times. The second result of the intrusion of the new men was also of great importance. Agricultural progress began. There is not at first much to record, but experiments began to be made ; these experiments and information on and suggestions for the conduct of agriculture began to be recorded by writers of the time, of whom the most famous was Gervoise Markham. Some of these books were widely read, but the farmers were slow to move. Still there was some improvement. Dry land was irrigated, and the drainage of wet land was sometimes undertaken. The drainage of the Fens, then a great area of over 1,000 square miles of marsh and lake, with islands like Ely standing out, was seriously attempted. The work had the support of the Duke of Bedford, who with thirteen friends initiated in 1630 a scheme for the drainage of Cambridgeshire : he employed a Dutchman, Vermuyden, to direct the work. Other schemes were started for the adjoining counties. Huge canals, or 'drains' as they are called still remaining, were cut across the county. The schemes were only partially successful and, at the time of the Civil War, the fenmen cut the banks of the drains and flooded much of the county. A century and a half later the work was recommenced and carried to a successful conclusion. In other directions there was substantial progress. The area under apples, pears, plums, cherries and other fruit was extended and more hops were grown. One writer describes a poultry farm in which a primitive form of incubator was used. Manuring was developed and, as a result of this and better cultivation, the yield of corn crops greatly increased. Turnips and clover were sown here and there on enclosed fields. Their use made it possible to keep land under cultivation year after year, instead of leaving it fallow every second or third year, and from this followed in a few generations a revolution in agricultural methods. Dairy farming was extending. Stock was also improving in quality. Progress would doubtless have been general had it not been for the feeling of insecurity that came over England with the acute political differences of the time. But notwithstanding this, agriculture definitely improved, and if the progress was not startling, it can at least be said that the way was being cleared for the beginning of the new agriculture which was developed in the two centuries that followed. The labourers, however, of whom there seemed to be an increasing number in these times, lost ground, for whilst prices as a rule went up, wages remained at about the old figures.

Before dealing in further detail with the events that belonged to the general stream of change, it will be well to refer to two special and peculiar events of the century, the Civil War and the Puritan movement.

Of these the first, the Civil War, the great political event of the century, seems, apart from the sense of insecurity it engendered, to have had comparatively little effect on rural life. It does not appear that the armies of either side devastated the country to any great extent. Of course, many men went from the villages to fight for Loyalists or for the Parliamentarians, according to their view of the great controversy. On the whole the squires, especially those of the old families, were on Charles's side, and in the early days of the struggle many of the peasants followed the squires. On the other hand, there were many Puritan yeomen and farmers, austere men, impressed with the new religious ideas, who followed Cromwell. But the main body of the country people remained at home, where, driven by need and interest, they ploughed, sowed and harvested their crops and pursued their ordinary occupations.

The spread of an aggressive form of Puritanism which took place during this century destroyed the boisterous good-nature of Elizabethan times, and broke up once for all much of the social life of the villages. Bull and bear baiting and other cruel sports were very properly stopped ; but the Puritans went further : maypoles were pulled down and old-fashioned village revels were suppressed, for dancing and acting were sin. Singing was supposed to be limited to psalm-singing, and the celebration of Christmas and other festivals was treated as superstition. Up to this time, Sunday, church once attended, had been a day devoted to every sort of amusement. But government intervened, a statute, in 1623,[1] forbade Sunday amusements, and later all persons were expressly forbidden under penalties to be present on 'the Lord's Day' at any wrestling, shooting, bowling, ringing of bells for pleasure, masques, wakes, church ales, dancing and other pastimes. The character of Sunday completely altered. Saints' days also ceased to be holidays, and to quote Markham, it was considered lawful 'to be well occupied on holy days.' The ideas which impelled this decay of social life, the encroachment on holidays and the introduction of Sabbatarianism, the greatest change perhaps in the country life of those times, can be well understood by a study of Bunyan's 'Pilgrim's Progress.' Bunyan was a man of the people and he understood the people. The gist of his teaching is clear enough. Put aside the things of the flesh, and consider only things of the spirit. But who is to be 'the Interpreter,' who shall say whether music, song and dancing, that give joy to life, are or are

*Puritanism and social life.*

[1] See Appendix, p. 176.

not of the spirit? The Puritan of the middle period of the century did not hesitate. Such things were banned, and although country people continued in many places their amusements on weekdays, and a social revival arose after the Restoration, the spirit of Merry England has never been fully restored to the villages.

Apart from these two special events, the century stands for a continual change in the general direction of the reconstruction already outlined.

Enclosures continued. Sometimes the small farmers gained by this process, sometimes they lost and were reduced to poverty, their fate varying **Enclosures.** according to whether the enclosures took the form of a fair division of land, creating many small holdings, or an appropriation of land by the lords of the manors and big farmers, and division into large farms. When they lost some wandered off, as had their predecessors in the XVIth century, to parishes where there were still large commons and, settling down, built cottages on the waste land and increased the class of squatters ; others took matters into their own hands, and joining their fellows in a band of 'Levellers' or 'Diggers,' destroyed the new hedges and filled up the ditches, hoping thereby to bring back the land to common use. Legislation and government inquiry on this subject went on to the middle of the century, since the government still viewed enclosures with some hostility, and fines were imposed on men who had enclosed. Common rights were, it appears, one of the questions at issue at the time of the Civil War. Undoubtedly, some of the country people who took part in the revolt against the Stuarts did so in the expectation that the Parliamentary party would, when in power, defend their rights to their commons. After the king's defeat, commoners are found laying their case before their new rulers. "By virtue of this conquest over the king," obtained by joint effort, they claim "freedom in the common lands," otherwise "we are," they say, "in a worse case than we were in the king's day." It does not seem that the Parliamentarians paid much attention to the claims of the commoners. Indeed, in the latter half of the century such bills as were introduced into Parliament on the subject favoured enclosures : opinion was not at that time so far altered as to secure the passing of these bills, but the view of the men in power was changing; and, from the middle of the century onwards, the government of the country, being largely influenced by commercial ideas and by the arguments of the large landholders, threw its influence on the side of the enclosers and appropriators of land. As a result the peasantry were left for nearly two hundred years to stand almost alone in their struggle for land and for the independence that went with it. Accordingly, enclosures went on apace. A new method was at that time invented by the lawyers whereby, the approval of many of the principal people in the manor having been obtained by persuasion or pressure, a suit in Chancery was commenced asking for enclosure, and an order for division of the estate made, without, it seems probable, consulting the wishes or convenience of the little people, whose only effective remedy was a subsequent costly appeal to the courts. In addition, the lords of the manor continued their enclosure of surplus waste land. By the time of the Reformation perhaps a quarter of England had been divided up into fenced fields.[1]

[1] See Appendix, pp. 164, 165.

The peasants had, in addition to the disappearance of many commons, one other loss. The English

**Sport and game.** country people have always been sportsmen, whilst game killed on the commons, woods and wastes must have been in mediaeval times an invaluable addition to the peasant farmers' larder. In the XIVth century it will be remembered the right to kill game was limited to the 40s. freeholder. It is doubtful whether this statute was enforced : indeed, before the time of police or gamekeepers it could hardly have been possible to prevent the peasantry snaring hares, ferreting rabbits or netting partridges on the great commons or in the woods and waste land. No one could have objected very seriously to such practices. But in the XVIIth century new conditions arose : game began to have a commercial value since wealthy people were buying considerable quantities of venison and other game. The class who were, as the century closed, securing the control of the country-side must have been fully aware of the change. They decided to secure for themselves the sporting rights, and Parliament was persuaded to pass a statute in 1670 [1] laying down the rule that no one was to kill game unless he had a freehold estate worth £100 a year or leasehold property worth £150. Thus game became substantially the property of the greater landholders.

Enclosures have always gone hand in hand with poverty, and it is not surprising to find that many

**Poverty and 'settlements.'** poor were to be found in the villages in this century while vagabonds were wandering all over the country. These unfortunate people continued to be a cause of endless

[1] See Appendix, p. 171.

trouble to the parish authorities responsible for their care. The law worked badly. The principle that the parish was to be responsible for its own poor sounds clear enough; but the application was not always easy. A woman might have been born in the West of England and lived all her life as the wife of a man residing in a Midland village: was she to go back to her place of birth before she could obtain relief? The members of an orphan family of pauper children might have been born in different villages: were they to be separated? This question of parish responsibility has been decided at different times in different manners. At one time it was laid down that the responsible parish was the pauper's place of birth; then the place in which he had settled for three years: later, the three years were reduced to one. As a natural effect of this legislation every parish wished to keep actual and prospective paupers from spending a year within its boundary and thus obtaining a 'settlement.' Every effort was made to keep poor people on the move. As time went on and the poor showed no signs of diminishing, the parishes felt they had not sufficient power to keep undesirable people outside their boundaries. To meet this view, Parliament passed in 1662 the Act of Settlement [1] which allowed the removal of any stranger, within forty days of his arrival, back to 'his own parish,' a phrase which was further explained to be one in which he had lived forty days. He was only to be allowed to stay if he could give security that he would never become chargeable to the parish. This act, although much modified by other statutes,[2] remained in force for over a century; it reintroduced a modified form of bondage, going far indeed towards reviving the old rule of astriction, under which

[1] See Appendix, p. 170.     [2] Ibid. pp. 170, 171.

in mediaeval times, the man had been bound to his manor. It also gave rise to a costly custom of carting the poor from place to place, in order that they might be dumped down in some parish that could be proved to be their birthplace, or place of settlement.

The country villages that lay on or near a road of any importance could not fail to be brought more into touch with the national life: for the **Travellers and the roads.** growth of the big cities and the development of trade between these cities and the market towns brought more people into the country. The travellers brought news and new ideas, whilst occasional newspapers, which the governments then published, must have reached the principal market towns.

There was considerable traffic on the roads. When the farmer had sold his corn, or wool or cloth, and in these times many men were farming no longer for food alone but had a definite surplus to sell, it would be loaded on pack-horses, or else carted away in great hooded waggons drawn by teams of eight horses. The villagers tramped, or, if they had a nag to ride, trotted off weekly to the market town and once or twice a year to a neighbouring fair. People of standing, both men and women, travelled on horseback, though occasionally a carriage may have been used; but such wheeled vehicles were strange sights outside the great towns. The roadways were unsuited for any large amount of traffic, being still mere strips of grass-land worn by the feet of the flocks and herds that passed along from time to time, and full of holes and ruts made by the farmers' carts and waggons. Travelling, too, was dangerous; armed ruffians haunted the woods and waste lands, and no one of any importance dared undertake a journey without an armed escort.

The travellers complained bitterly of the state of the roads, and pressure was constantly being put on the parishes through which the principal roads ran to put them into some sort of repair. Very little was, however, done, the proper method of making a hard road being entirely unknown in England, whilst even if the people of the villages had known how to make one, it is doubtful if they would have undertaken it. The parish only wanted to get to the nearest market town, and they naturally evaded the duty of repairing the high roads for the benefit of the traders and other travellers from the cities. As a rule, the roads seemed to have remained in the state of decay in which they had been for many generations. Probably, however, some of the great main roads were kept in better repair. Certainly an attempt was made to get the Great North Road patched up, and in 1663 [1] the justices were authorized to set up toll-bars and make a charge for those who went along this road, so that the users might contribute to the costs of the repairs. This idea was not a new one: tolls charged to passengers over bridges, to be employed in their repair, had been common enough from the earliest times: but this seems to have been the first occasion such a scheme was applied to roads. It was a first step towards the turnpike system which was adopted throughout England in the following centuries.

At the beginning of the century the Church, which had in Tudor times already lost much of its influence and

[1] See Appendix, p. 173.

also much of its hold over the imagination of the villagers, was suffering from internal difficulties, due largely to the growth of the Presbyterian movement. Early in the century writers told of a group of people standing outside the church, called the 'Children of Light,' the name first assumed by the Society which afterwards took the title of 'The Friends,' and was derisively called 'The Quakers.' Independents and Baptists also came into prominence as the century progressed. Finally, members of these and of other religious bodies became completely detached from the National Church. This occurred in 1662, when the Act of Uniformity[1] laid down that no one could hold a living who was not prepared to give 'unfeigned assent and consent' to the contents of the Anglican Prayer Book. As a result, some 2,000 ministers of religion, who had at that time charge of parishes, gave up their positions and withdrew from the National Church; from that time onward the religious life of the country districts has been divided into two sections, the Anglicans and the Nonconformists. The Anglican preachers and divines of ability of that time collected in the towns, whilst the country parsons seem to have been poor and ill-educated and to have attached themselves more and more to the ruling families, the country squires; as this tendency developed the Established Church finally ceased to have the democratic character noticeable in the Middle Ages. This alliance between squire and parson resulted in the latter attaining a definite social position in the village : he belonged to the gentry, and thus became even further detached from the people as a whole. On the other hand, some, at least, of the Nonconformist bodies from

The Church and Nonconformity.

[1] See Appendix, p. 176.

the very first took a more democratic line, and gathered within their organizations a considerable number of the more intelligent and active of the villagers, from which class some of their ministers and lay preachers have been recruited.

The general character of the country life of the century has now, it is hoped, been made clear. The
country-side was slowly changing : more and

**General character of the changes.** more land was being enclosed, and more and more were the farmers of enterprise experimenting and succeeding and coming
to the front : but such men rarely rose into the upper class, for the new landlords had consolidated their position and were building up the great estates and ' settling' them on the families which were to control rural England for many a generation. Meanwhile, the villagers were losing their gaiety. Some, too, were losing their land, and were being crushed down into the great pauper class, which was by that time under the control of the law. The Church, too, had lost its grip on village life, and a new element of independent thought was spreading. A way was being prepared for the greater changes that were to follow with the Industrial and Social Revolution of the XVIIIth and XIXth centuries.

# CHAPTER VIII

## THE SOCIAL REVOLUTION OF THE XVIIITH CENTURY

AFTER the fall of the Stuarts comes a period of about a century and a half during which England took the form in which we see it to-day—the industrial England of great towns and great enterprises and rural England, with, for its main features, privately owned land, large enclosed farms, capitalist farmers, a large class of labourers and a highly developed agricultural system.

This phase of the reconstruction could hardly have occurred so rapidly as it did, had not the government of the country, in Parliament, in the counties, and, to a large extent, in the villages themselves, been, from the Revolution onwards, in the main in the hands of the 'landed gentry'; this class retained their control over central government until the passing of the Reform Bill in 1832, and over local government for another half-century. The 'landed gentry,' it will be remembered, were sprung partly from the aristocratic families, partly from such peasant families as had become enriched, but largely also from the lawyers, merchants and other business men who, from Tudor times onwards, had been

*The control of power and the squirearchy.*

drifting from the towns to the villages, to secure there the coveted position of county families.

From the wealthier of the landed gentry came the members of Parliament, since a statute passed in 1710 [1] had decreed that only landowners could sit in Parliament, whilst the enormous expenses connected with parliamentary elections and public life made it a career open only to men who had command of great wealth. The management of local affairs became vested in the same hands, almost all the powers that had been in the hands of the various bodies, in which the people had a voice, being by the XVIIIth century gathered into the hands of the justices of the peace. Only the parish, in its vestry assembled, continued as a democratic organization, and the transaction of its business was, in practice, subject to the control of the local landholders and justices. Indeed, before the end of the XVIIIth century the entire administration of county affairs, save the management of those roads which were in the hands of turnpike trusts, as well as the ultimate authority in parish affairs, rested substantially in the hands of the landed gentry. Moreover, more and more, all business, whether county government or administration of justice, was carried on in private, so that the public lost all control. In addition to the administration of the law and of public affairs, the justices also initiated and administered regulations relating to housing and to wages, matters in some respects affecting the lives of the people more profoundly than did the laws themselves. The county families were, in fact, supreme, for they controlled not only the laws and their administration, but the lives of the people. They consolidated their power by con-

[1] See Appendix, p. 167.

tinuing the system of land settlement whereby the great estates remained in the same families from generation to generation, by absorbing into their class the wealthy merchants, lawyers, and other townspeople who might, under other circumstances, have formed a strong body of opposition to their control ; and by securing for their class government the support of the large farmers, of the clergy, and of the country lawyers, who might, if their interest had not been concerned, have been severe critics of their administrative methods.

The gathering of the control of power into the hands of this small section of the community resulted in one great evil. So little consideration was given by the new rulers to the interests of the small peasant farmers and labourers, that the men of these classes were allowed to sink down, until by the early years of the XIXth century they were in a condition of poverty and misery which, having regard to the wealth of England at that time, has no precedent in the history of the English workers on the land. But it does not follow that the English country squires are to be subjected to an unqualified condemnation. The course they took was the outcome of their character, and this period cannot be understood unless this character is grasped. Generous and hospitable, good-natured when their interests were not concerned, devoted to sport, adventure and pleasure, fond of controlling the lives and affairs of others, the English squires of the XVIIIth century carried on the public work of the country-side with considerable energy and some ability. But the value of their very activity was largely destroyed by the defects of their temperaments. For these men were almost always narrow, and were usually imbued with a considerable amount of arrogance and prejudice. They were limited in their work by their ignorance of political science and also by an extraordinary want of understanding of the lives and the thoughts, not only of other nations, but of the men of their own nation who lay outside their own class. There is a further point to bear in mind. To them the county nobility and gentry and their tenants, the leasehold farmers, stood for England, and the squires held that if these classes were to go, the country would be lost ; to their minds the interest of other sections of society was a subsidiary matter. For a country squire to legislate and to control government in the interests of his class must have seemed the most natural thing in the world. By advancing his own class he was in his view advancing England. It was this point of view, coupled with their want of human understanding, that made the squires so arbitrary in the exercise of the power vested in them.

The first outcome of the new control was the carrying of the Corn Bounty Act of 1688.[1]  This act gave a bounty of 5s. a quarter on exported wheat, so long as the home price did not exceed 48s. a quarter, and made similar regulations for barley, oats, peas, etc. At the same time, import duties remained high.[1]  These laws seem to have had some satisfactory results. The price of corn continued for the best part of a century at a moderate level, which afforded a reasonable and steady profit for farmers. The cultivator was thus encouraged to farm his land well, to employ improved methods, and to bring more land into cultivation. The importation of stock from abroad being completely forbidden, the farmer was also able to obtain the full benefit of the improved

Corn laws.

[1] See Appendix, p. 172.

demand for beef, mutton and pork, which grew with
the enlarged town population. As a general result, production was encouraged, and for about one hundred
years England was able to supply her own food, and
even in favourable seasons to export some corn. From
the closing years of the XVIIIth century England
ceased to feed herself and became an importing country ;
this change, coupled with the higher import duties on
wheat and the Napoleonic wars, resulted in a rise in the
price of corn. The high prices were accompanied by
great variations from year to year ; wheat, in particular,
oscillated from under 50s. a quarter to 156s. The
high prices were a serious misfortune for the manual
workers both in town and country, since they resulted
in a great increase in the cost of food. Amongst the
farmers, the clever men made considerable fortunes; but
the class as a whole benefited less than might be expected,
since rents went up and rates were extremely high,
whilst the variations in prices introduced a disastrous
element of uncertainty and speculation into farming.

The next important result of the new control was the
development of cultivation—the uprising of the new
agriculture. It was typical of the XVIIth
century that much information and advice
was given to farmers by many ingenious
writers. In the XVIIIth century this
advice began to be taken to heart and agriculture
improved steadily.

The new agri-
culture and
its leaders.

The story of this improvement can best be told by
reference to the lives of its most distinguished leaders,
men who made this period famous and unique in
English history. Of these the first was Jethro Tull
(1674–1741). A lawyer by training, he gave up his

profession and settled down, as quite a young man, on his father's farm at Howberry in Oxfordshire. He seems at once to have thrown himself into farming, and some two years later he was inventing and using a clover drill, planned on the general lines of the implement used at the present day. He developed this drill, adapting it for corn and turnips, and claimed that he could make savings on a large scale, not only in the amount of seed sown, but in labour in sowing and in cultivation. He advocated the increased use of turnips and clover, and emphasized the importance of keeping the land clean and free from weeds, which could of course be more easily done when the crop was sown in lines with a drill than when scattered broadcast. He published in 1731 a book dealing with many of these matters under the title of " Horse-hoeing Husbandry." His proposals were much discussed, but rarely adopted in his lifetime, and he himself died ruined.

A more influential and immediately successful leader was Lord Townshend (1674-1738), a contemporary of Tull. He started life as a politician and diplomat, taking a leading and brilliant part in the intricate political life of the first thirty years of the century ; but in 1730 he threw up his political career and retired to his Norfolk estates, to see what he could do to reclaim the stretches of marsh, waste and woodland of which a great part of his property consisted. In this work he was extraordinarily successful. Townshend treated his sandy wastes with marl to such good account, that he transformed them into fertile fields and made a fortune. It became a saying in Norfolk that " He who marls sand may buy his land." Even more important than this development of marling was the spread of the cultivation of turnips, clover and other grasses for which Townshend, nicknamed "Turnip Townshend," was largely responsible. His land was thus kept under permanent cultivation, since instead of fallowing he alternated roots and corn, thus creating the Norfolk four-course system. Wheat is followed in this course by turnips or other roots ; then comes barley or oats, followed by clover or other grasses. Townshend found that the green crops fed off by sheep, or stored for winter food for stock, resulted in improved sheep and stock. At the same time the ground, being fertilized by the sheep's droppings or by the farmyard manure, produced better corn crops. This method of treatment of the land helped in every way. It meant better crops, better sheep and better stock. This system could not be carried out on the old-fashioned open fields, so long as it was the custom for everyone's cattle to stray over the land after the crops were off, since, if any one farmer had been so enterprising as to produce a crop of turnips or clover, the flocks and herds would all be found browsing on his land until the crop had been devoured. But on enclosed farms the system was adopted with great success, and not only Townshend, a great advocate of enclosures, but many of the farmers who followed him made fortunes. Landowners as well as farmers benefited, for rents increased rapidly.

What Townshend did for field cultivation, Bakewell (1725–94) did for sheep. Bakewell, who belonged to a later generation than Tull and Townshend, was a typical John Bull, a big, burly, rosy-faced man, with breeches, boots, red waistcoat and loose coat. He lived at Dishley, near Loughborough, in simple style, and the celebrities and nonentities, from home and abroad who collected at his farm, were entertained without ceremony in his kitchen. It was Bakewell who systematized stock-breeding, though it was only with sheep that he was permanently successful. He created the new Leicester breed, and his rams went all over England to improve the breed of English sheep. It was said of him that he gave England two pounds of mutton where it had one pound before. He treated all his animals with kindness and kept them scrupulously clean. Although he is most famous as a sheep-breeder, he also bred cattle and horses and was a great advocate of irrigation: on his own farm he made a canal 1¼ miles long for the purpose of flooding his meadows and producing rich crops of grass.

Many farmers have followed in the steps of Bakewell, but of the men of that time the most famous was Charles Colling (1751–1836). Bakewell had taught Colling the importance of good stock, and Colling applied Bakewell's ideas to cattle-breeding; his great success was made with his shorthorns.

While Bakewell and Colling were typical yeomen, Coke of Norfolk (1752–1842) represented a different class. He was a man of property, and when, as a young man of twenty-four, he succeeded to the great estate of Holkham in Norfolk, he had ample wealth at his command; he was thus able to take advantage of all the knowledge and experience of the pioneers. Over the greater part of his estate there was, when he came into possession, no wheat, nor roots, clover or grasses: only a few poor sheep straggled over the rough land. Two years later, in 1778, he commenced farming on his own account; he is said to have spent half a million pounds in reclaiming his land; and so successful was he that, whilst his tenant farmers flourished, they were yet able to pay greatly increased rents, so that his rent-roll went up from a few thousands a year to many thousands. His methods, then new, now seem obvious. To his land he applied marl, clay and manures. He drained and irrigated, and when the land was brought into condition he sowed seed with drills and kept it clean. He introduced wheat in place of rye, and used to boast that he had changed West Norfolk from a rye-producing to a wheat-growing district. He farmed with the improved rotation of crops—growing turnips, clover and other roots and grasses. He bred the best class of stock, particularly South Down sheep and Devon cattle. His tenants were treated extremely well, provided they farmed well. A man of great power, energy and personal attraction, Coke, 'the handsome Englishman,' was one of the most famous figures of his time. He entered Parliament in 1776 as member for Norfolk, and remained in the House of Commons with two intervals until the Reform Parliament of 1832. In 1837 he was made Earl of Leicester. Holkham and its master were for many years one of the sights of England, to be visited not only by all the great personages of our country, but also by those from abroad who came to England in that time. He kept open house on the occasion of his annual sheep-shearings, and at the last of these functions, which was held in 1821, it was said that 7,000 people took part.

There was one other man of the time who had remarkable influence. Arthur Young (1741–1820), who ultimately became Secretary of the first Board of Agriculture (a semi-official body founded in 1795 and dissolved in 1822), started life as a farmer; he very quickly failed, probably because of his unlimited enthusiasm for experiment. Having failed at farming, he set to work as an investigator and writer. He travelled first throughout England and later in France, and recorded in a number of books, which attained a great reputation, the results of his inquiries. Young, who was perhaps the greatest English writer on agriculture, spent his life exciting the interest and enthusiasm of the people of the country in its development, and his propagandist work ably supplemented the more practical work of other leaders.

The lives of these men tell incidentally the story of the new agriculture. The introduction of laboursaving machines, the spread of clover and turnips, the development of the four-course system of farming, the enormous improvement in the quality of stock, combined with the habit of research to revolutionize agriculture; at the same time, in order to carry out the new system, the capitalist took the place of the small man working on his own land.

The new agriculture meant, of course, a large increase in production : and so farmers of the new school had a considerable surplus over what they needed for their home consumption. There was an increasing amount of corn, and more stock to send to market or to sell to dealers buying for the town demand. The farmers, when they had sold their produce, became in their turn buyers on an increased scale, for they had money to spend on such articles as they needed for their improved standard of living, and for the effective cultivation of their farms.

*Business and social intercourse and sport.*

The trade so created attached itself to the country towns, by this time well established as the centres of

time, energy and money for what was substantially the public benefit. As a result the old form of way held its own throughout England, though here and there was found a new type which arose in this century—the causeway-road, consisting of the old belt of rough grass-land with a stone causeway about a yard and a half broad. On this causeway travellers rode and pack-horses tramped, whilst on the grass the waggons ploughed their way and the stock of all sorts straggled along to some great town or market. During all this period the country's internal trade grew steadily. To meet this increase and the difficulties of transport, canals, then new to England, were extended throughout the country until the advent of railways in the XIXth century : they greatly reduced cost of transit and gave considerable impulse to the trade in agricultural produce of the districts they served. But the roads remained the main arteries of distribution : and the increase of traffic tended to make them worse. Parliament devised two remedies. The first, a singularly ineffective one, the regulation by statute [1] of the size of cartwheels and the number of horses to be harnessed to each waggon, was attempted in order to reduce the damage to the roads done by carts and waggons. The second remedy was the setting up of bodies to put and keep in order some particular road or the roads of a district. These bodies, called Turnpike Trusts, were administered by trustees appointed by the government.

Turnpike trusts [2] were first formed early in the XVIIIth century, and increased until ultimately the number of such bodies reached over 1,000, with responsibility for some 23,000 miles of road. They had commonly the widest powers to make or to close roads and to regu-

[1] See Appendix, p. 173.    [2] Ibid. pp. 173, 174.

late traffic, and also to make levies for labour and material on the parishes through which the roads passed. They had also the right to erect their turnpikes or barriers at various places across the roads, where tolls were collected by the pikemen. Notwithstanding the formation of these trusts the greater number of the roads of England were little changed, for they remained under parish control until the XIXth century, and the parishes could not be persuaded to make new roads or even to carry out effective repairs. As the turnpike trusts increased, here and there in England, for the first time since the withdrawal of the Romans, hard roads were to be found, on which all could travel without fear of accident. To these roads definite boundaries were given, as the process of enclosure continued. At the same time quarter sessions gave better attention to the repair of the bridges that carried the principal roads. Travel became easier, especially when the introduction of stage coaches followed the creation of new roads. As an example of this change, it is interesting to know that in 1739 there was a good hard road from London to Grantham, and no doubt this road was a little later extended to Edinburgh, as a stage-coach service was opened between London and that town in 1754. In the latter part of the century the better managed trusts began to appoint skilled surveyors, who built more and more of these hard roads running down the centres of the old grassways: whilst finally, in the XIXth century, the famous roadmakers Macadam and Telford appeared on the scene.

The turnpike trust system can hardly be considered a great success: there was often the grossest mismanagement. In many cases the trusts delegated their duties: in the latter years of the century the

roads were very often farmed out at so much a year
to contractors, and the right to take the tolls was
sold by auction to speculators. Nevertheless turnpike
trusts were a step ahead of parish management, for it
is extremely unlikely that the parishes would ever have
made the hard roads of England. Without hard roads
there would have been no stage coaches, and far less of
that coming and going of people that did much to draw
the country together and create a feeling of national
unity.

The effect of the new control and the new agriculture
on the life of the village is far less satisfactory than its
result on the cultivation of the soil. At the
**Enclosure.** beginning of the XVIIIth century the
enclosures and the open fields were still
found side by side. Perhaps a quarter of England was
already in fenced fields, a third in open arable fields,
meadows, and pasture common, and the balance in woodlands, wastes, moor and fens.[1] With the two systems
went the different classes of cultivators, the enclosed fields
tending to pass more and more into the hands of the prosperous larger leasehold tenants, who depended on hired
labour; the open fields being in the main farmed by
small farmers, most of whom were, at that time, also
doing well, particularly when they added to their profits
by weaving, spinning and other industries. Below
the farmers was an increasing class of labourers, many
of whom were squatters on the commons, where they
had erected their own cottages; these men, even if they
depended in the main for their livelihood on wages,
commonly, at that time, had a little land of their own,
or, at least, by custom if not by law, common rights for

[1] See Appendix, pp. 164, 165.

their cows, sheep, pigs or fowls. Below them, again, was a definite pauper class, not so large as it ultimately became. There was doubtless, in most parishes in England, some open and some enclosed land, and also some individuals of all classes, landlords, big leasehold farmers, peasant farmers, labourers with land or common rights, and a few poverty-stricken wretches : but the proportion differed. Nevertheless, in most places, there must have been at that time, as there had been in the XVth century, a practical ladder whereby a man could work his way upwards from the labouring class to the position of a considerable farmer.

But this condition could not be maintained. There was a widespread demand for enclosures, especially from the landlords and larger farmers. This demand, doubtless, appeared to these classes to be justified by the nation's experience, since undoubtedly such enclosures as had already taken place had resulted in better crops, improved stock, higher rents and increased tithes. The new agriculture certainly seemed to demand enclosure for its growth, and it is not therefore surprising that enclosure in all its forms continued. The sorting out of the scattered strips amongst the tenants, the fencing in of the land when the strips had been sorted into blocks, and the enclosing of parts of the common fields, by some sort of agreement, went steadily on. Moreover, the larger appropriations by the lords of the manors and other landholders of commons and of woodlands, wastes and fenlands must have continued. Of the land which had remained open at the beginning of the XVIIIth century, the greater part, perhaps two-thirds, was dealt with in one or other of these ways.

But the remainder of the unenclosed land was treated

by new methods. Enclosure by Act of Parliament began, and in the XVIIIth century became a usual way of procedure. At first these enclosures by Act of Parliament were a rarity, but later on they became a common practice. In all, before the middle of the XIXth century there were some four thousand special Acts of Parliament [1] (including special awards under general acts), and these accounted for the dividing up of some six million acres of open arable fields, meadows, commons, woods and wastes. The method pursued to obtain these statutory enclosures, and their results, requires careful consideration. These enclosures were secured by bills relating to some particular area, and were carried through Parliament on, as a rule, the initiative of a local lord of the manor, or other big landholder, with whom were sometimes associated the rector or vicar of the parish, and perhaps some big farmers and other local persons who were prepared to support the scheme. The act, when passed, ordered the redivision and fencing in of such open arable land and lot meadows, commons, woods or wastes as were included in the scheme of the act, and appointed commissioners to carry out this division. In the settlement in Parliament of the provisions of these statutes the small farmers and the labourers had little or no voice. As a result, their interests were neglected. It is therefore not surprising to learn that the enthusiasm amongst the new agriculturists for these statutory enclosures found no response among the smaller men. Their attitude is well expressed by a passage from the *Annual Register* for 1797, which referred in the following words to one of those occasions on which the peasantry had succeeded in making their voices heard : "On

[1] See Appendix, p. 169.

any might clim|
labourer and fa

In the latter
the XIXth cent
            mass
**The labourers** beer
**and poverty.**
            out
the loss of thei
this class had, e
istics that had
ancestors.  The
had belonged to
longer cheerful
observed.  In ma
save Christmas
the village sick
tion, a relic of
and spent at t
its corporate s
the democratic
of the people;
leader of their l
the squirearchy
bodies grew in
their organizat
thinkers among
whole the Nor
tion, and whils
did little for s

The labourer
large section w
of paupers.  F
birth or of the

Tuesday evening a great number of farmers were
observed going along Pall Mall with cockades in their
hats.  On inquiring the reason, it appeared that they
all lived in or near the parish of Stanwell in the county
of Middlesex, and they were returning to their wives
and families to carry them the agreeable news of a
bill being rejected for enclosing the said common,
which, if carried into execution, might have been the
ruin of a great number of families."  The belief of these
Middlesex farmers that enclosures brought ruin to a
great number of families appears to have been founded
on a somewhat bitter experience, for undoubtedly
these statutory enclosures, whilst ultimately improving
the conditions under which agriculture was carried
on, too often reduced the small peasant farmers to
the position of labourers without land or common
rights.  If the procedure employed in the passing of
the acts gave no opportunity to the peasantry to
express their views on a matter on which their whole
lives depended, the procedure on the actual division
of the land by the commissioners was a still greater
grievance.  The small holders of land and common
rights, farmers or labourers, had, in the first instance,
to put their claims into a legal form.  The law had
long since (in Gateward's case in 1603), decided that
common rights did not belong to persons merely
because they inhabited a village, or manor, but that the
rights went with special plots of land.  These rights
had to be proved strictly, and this was, to many,
an impossible task.  But even if the peasants proved
their rights and secured a piece of land in compensation
for their losses, the plot was, in general, subjected to
the payment of a share of the expenses of the Act
of Parliament and of the commissioners and surveyors:

more
cond
able
the
what
or  t
with
You
from
teen
injur
of  N
been
the  r
these
may
had
from
  Th
enclo
men
holdi
or  at
same
farm
bone
large
daily
other
have
cultu
was
obser
comp

sible, and the ratepayers of every parish lived in fear of the pauper who might secure a 'settlement,' and so did their utmost to prevent poor people settling down within their boundaries. Landlords pulled down cottages and prevented new ones being built. Parishes spent fortunes in lawsuits amongst themselves on the question of liability to support individual paupers, and although the provisions of the Act of Settlement were modified by the act passed in 1795,[1] which forbade the removal of any individual from one parish to another unless he was in actual want, much money was spent in carting poor people back to their own parishes. In 1815 the parishes of England spent over a quarter of a million pounds on such litigation and removals.

Indeed, during the latter part of the XVIIIth century the condition of the poor became more and more miserable, especially as the rural iron trade, the cloth trade and other village industries, decayed with the uprising of the factory towns. The people suffered greatly as the price of wheat, and therefore of food, went up. In 1795 there were widespread food riots, in many cases directed by women. At some places crowds of women seized the corn and other produce and proceeded to sell it at what they considered fair prices, paying the amount received—the fair price—to the owners. Social reformers in Parliament introduced proposals for securing a legal minimum wage for working people, but the *laissez-faire* theories of Adam Smith had such a hold on men's minds at that time that any proposal of this character had no chance of success. Action was taken, however, without special legislation, in 1795, the outcome of a meeting of magistrates and clergy held at Speenhamland in Buckingham-

[1] See Appendix, p. 171.

shire, to give special consideration to the relief of the poor. Recommendations were then made for securing a definite wage for working people, and these recommendations were not only adopted in that county, but in the course of the next forty years spread, with modifications, right through the counties of England, excepting only Northumberland and Durham. The scheme adopted at Speenhamland was as follows:—A scale of wages was drawn up, varying according to the price of bread. For example, when the gallon loaf of seconds flour weighing 8 pounds 11 ounces cost 1s., a man was held to be entitled to receive 3s. a week for himself, 1s. 6d. a week for his wife, and the same for each child. Such a man would, therefore, when the gallon loaf cost 1s., be entitled, if he had a wife and four children, to 10s. 6d. a week and, if the price of bread was higher, the wages went up in proportion. Who, then, was to see that the man received his due wage? The responsibility was placed on the parish, and the labourer who was out of work had to apply to the overseer, whose duty it was to secure him employment. Sometimes the men collected on Saturdays and were put up for auction amongst the employers, going to the highest bidder. Sometimes they were sent from house to house, 'on the rounds,' as it was called, asking for work. The farmers who secured the men paid them a low wage, perhaps 6d. to 1s. a day : the balance fell on the parish rates, out of which the wages were supplemented to make the total amount up to the scale figure. The introduction of such drastic new regulations without the need of special legislation is an astonishing instance of the power of the justices of the peace.

This system was naturally accompanied by a con-

siderable rise in rates, which are said to have doubled
in the first fifteen years of the XIXth century, but
the gain to the farmers in reduced wages must have
counterbalanced their increased rates, or the system
could hardly have continued, as it did, for about forty
years.    But if farmers benefited, labourers lost; we see,
indeed, the rapid degradation of almost the whole of
the latter class.    To illustrate the effect of this system.
It was almost hopeless for a man who was not willing to
become a pauper, to obtain work, for to live he must
receive full wage from the farmer; this the latter would
not be prepared to give, as he could hire a pauper for
much less.    Everyone, therefore, tended to drift into the
pauper class.    Again, under the regulations, the larger
the family the more a man earned.    As a result there
was no inducement to restraint or thrift and the pauper
population increased rapidly.    The position of an
unmarried man or of a young married man with a
wife and, for example, one child, would be the worst,
as the wages might be only 3s. or 6s. a week
respectively.

The outcome of this system was seen not only in the
increase in the number of paupers, but also in the rapid
growth of poaching and stealing.    Poaching, both for
food and for trade, was a recognized country custom
before the days of the Speenhamland system of parish
doles in aid of wages.    Parliament was concerned about
it in 1770,[1] when new punishments were laid down for
poachers, the justices being authorized to give twelve
months' imprisonment and a public whipping for a
second offence.    But men whose wages were only a few
shillings a week and who had perhaps a wife and
child to support were not deterred by these penalties.

[1] See Appendix, p. 171.

The practice grew, and the justices' time was constantly occupied with these cases. In the year 1800 [1] Parliament increased the penalties, and the justices were authorized to send all poachers over twelve years of age into the army or navy.

Bread was at that time dearer, and the custom of game-preserving had greatly increased the number of pheasants. Thus the temptation to poach was greater than ever : this temptation the half-starved labourers were unable to resist, and poaching continued on a large scale, the birds being collected by the stage coaches and carriers' carts for the markets of London and other great towns. A large and well recognized trade in poached game sprang up. Indeed, in the early days of the XIXth century, it could have been no easy thing to find an able-bodied labourer who was not a poacher.

There was, at that time, no body of police able to deal with these infringements of the game laws, and their enforcement was left to the squires and their keepers. As a result, there was in many districts open war between the poachers and the keepers. The poachers formed gangs, and when these gangs came into contact with the keepers there would be a scuffle, and it was not rare for men on either side to be killed. Legislation was especially directed against these gangs,[1] and any poachers who showed fight against keepers were liable to be hanged.[2] Nevertheless, the spur of hunger was strong. Poaching continued, and for the first thirty years of the XIXth century the game laws were the cause, in a large part of England, of a most bitter feeling between the squire and the village.

[1] See Appendix, p. 171.                    [2] Ibid. p. 172.

This, then, was the outcome of the rise and control of the squirearchy. The completion of the redistribution of the land into enclosed fields, the creation of a new and improved system of farming, the abolition of the peasant farmer and the rearrangement of the agricultural classes, with an impoverished and discontented labouring class at the base. Then there gradually emerged the typical XIXth century village community, with its business basis and its three main clear-cut classes—the landlords, the tenant farmers and the labourers.

**General conclusions.**

# PART III

## *RECONSTRUCTED RURAL ENGLAND*

### (ABOUT 1800–1914)

## CHAPTER IX

### THE NINETEENTH CENTURY
#### (*Before the Agricultural Catastrophe*)

IT is important to realize clearly that already, at the beginning of the century, England had ceased to be a predominantly agricultural country. At that time, indeed, only about a third of our population was engaged in the cultivation of the land, and England's main interest was directed to manufacture and trade: moreover, during the whole of the century the proportion of the country people to townspeople steadily diminished. We are, therefore, now considering the history of a comparatively small and diminishing section of the English people.

*Agriculture and industry.*

Although estates of the old manorial form were still common in many counties at the beginning of the XIXth century, and have continued in some places up to the present time, enclosure went on so rapidly in the earlier years, that by 1820 rural England had become in the main a country of enclosed fields, owned by landlords and cultivated by tenant farmers. Of these

*The establishment of the new system.*

farmers about half must have been what are now called small holders, men who tilled the land with the help of their wives and families, while the other farmers were large holders, employing hired labourers.

The development of this characteristic XIXth century system of landlord, leasehold tenant and hired labourer, working on enclosed farms, brought with it further great improvements in farm buildings and in agricultural machinery and implements, changes for the better in character of stock, heavier crops and continuous cropping, and, indeed, progress in agriculture in every direction. This progress was largely due to the considerable amount of capital spent on the land by landlords and tenant farmers.

The new system was of necessity accompanied by the general adoption of the lease or agreement, designed to fix the rent to be paid by the tenant, and to lay down the conditions for the cultivation of the land. These rents and conditions have, of course, varied throughout England from time to time as prices and other conditions have changed.[1]

Class relationships.

One might expect to find difficulties arising out of the conflict of interests between landlords and tenants, created by the leasehold system so regulated, but as a matter of fact there has been little serious friction. This was due, in the first instance, to certain special conditions prevailing in England. The landlords and farmers, it should be observed, had a common interest in keeping up the price of corn and stock. These prices the landed gentry, during the period that they controlled Parliament, were able to regulate by adjust-

[1] See Appendix, p. 166.

ing import duties. From the time, towards the close of the XVIIIth century, when England ceased to produce sufficient corn for her own consumption, this regulation of prices became a potent force in rural life. Numerous Acts of Parliament, the Corn Laws [1] as they were called, were passed in the first half of the century to limit importation of corn and keep up prices—and there were also similar duties on stock. Now it is obvious that this regulation of prices by legislation, carried with it the power to make or mar the career of every farmer in the country, and so served to attach the farmers to their landlords by a strong bond of interest. The policy of import duties was attacked by the town politicians, and a strong movement, the Anti-Corn-Law League, founded in Manchester in 1838, carried on a well organized and effective agitation until the introduction of Free Trade in corn in 1846.[2] Against this movement landlords and farmers stood, as a rule, shoulder to shoulder. This alliance, strengthened as it often was by personal friendship and other social considerations, and cemented by the assistance generously given by landlords to their tenants on many occasions in times of difficulty, outlived the abolition of the corn laws and became a tradition in the English country-side. Farmers and landlords, the modern representatives of the two classes that were almost at war in the XIVth century, generally stood together in the XIXth. As a result England has been free from the struggles between these two classes that served to embitter Irish rural life. But this alliance had another effect, for it often meant that these two classes combined to oppose the interests of the labourers. A clear understanding of these points throws

[1] See Appendix, pp. 172, 173.          [2] Ibid. p. 173.

light on many incidents in the last century, the true meaning of which would otherwise be difficult to grasp.

Between the employers and labourers, however, the system has never worked smoothly, since it created at the base of the social structure a mass of impoverished and discontented men, the 'labouring poor' as they were called, who seem from the very beginning to have bitterly resented their subservient position. This discontent made itself conspicuous in the riots and risings that occurred in the year 1830, and later on in the great Agricultural Labourers' Trade Union movement, which, founded in 1872, was carried on for some years under the direction of Joseph Arch.

The conditions of agriculture varied greatly from time to time during the century. In the first fifteen years, owing to the Napoleonic **Agricultural conditions in outline.** Wars and the stringent character of the corn laws of the time, wheat averaged about 85s. a quarter and sometimes almost doubled that price; at the same time there was a high price for stock. As a result farmers flourished and landlords secured high rents, whilst labourers eked out their miserable wages by allowances under the Speenhamland regulations, which they supplemented by poaching and stealing. Enclosures by statute and by appropriation continued rapidly. There was a rush to buy land. Speculation was widespread. Many of the remaining peasant proprietors sold out, whilst others borrowed on mortgage and bought more land and sometimes lost all. The prosperous times came to an end in 1816, the 'black year,' which gave one of the worst harvests ever known. Subsequently, owing in part to bad weather, in part to the over-speculation, and in part to the high rents that had been fixed in the good times, there was a period of great depression, and landlords, farmers and labourers suffered together. As a result rents dropped. Then again the tide turned, and during the first forty years of the Victorian era there was a time of general prosperity for both farmers and landlords. Wheat during this time averaged about 53s. a quarter ; this was lower than it had been, but the improvements of every description that came into widespread use during these years, marked as they were by many good seasons, resulted in the saving of labour and increase of production, and so in good profits for farmers. Rents again went up, reaching their highest figures about 1879, three or four years after the tide had turned against the farmers. Whilst farmers and landlords flourished, labourers continued to live in great poverty, although they managed to slightly improve their position. In 1875 a series of bad seasons commenced and the period of agricultural prosperity drew to a close.

It is easy to get a good idea of the condition of agriculture and of the farmer's life in the enclosed districts, early in the century, by a study of Arthur Young's ' County Surveys.' His report on Hertfordshire, for example, which he visited in 1801, provides us with much information. Almost all Hertfordshire was by that time enclosed, and let out to tenant farmers in farms of, as a rule, from 150 to 400 acres, though there were some larger and many less. Rents and tithes, which latter, though then commuted in this county, were still paid by the farmer, averaged together, Young

**Agriculture at the beginning of the century.**

thought, about 18s. 6d. an acre.   Poor rates, then
going up rapidly, were perhaps 5s. an acre.   The
farmers on an average were then paying under these
heads about 23s. 6d. an acre, which would not differ
greatly from the amount they paid at the end of the
century.   Rents were, however, inclined to go up.
Most of the land in Hertfordshire was in those days
under the plough.   Much wheat was grown, and the
crop varied from 20 bushels to 40 bushels an acre,
not very much less than the yield of modern times;
the English average at the close of the century being
about 32 bushels an acre.   The price, however, was
much higher then than later; in 1801 it averaged about
120s. a quarter, as against 26s. 9d. in 1901.   Besides
wheat, Young found oats, barley, peas and beans in
general cultivation, whilst turnips and clover (currently
reported to have been introduced into the county by
Oliver Cromwell) and tares were in widespread use.
Some farmers were also growing sainfoin and swedes,
whilst cabbage, potatoes, trefoil, lucerne and carrots
were novelties as field crops, only to be found on a
few farms.

The Norfolk four-course system was common at
that time—wheat, and then turnips, followed by barley
and clover—and the old system of fallowing the land
between corn crops was being given up wherever
possible.

A great deal of attention was given to manuring
land, and bush draining, paring and burning, and
irrigation are referred to as being used with success
in some places.

The principal breeds of sheep were Southdown,
Wiltshire, Cotswold and Leicester, and amongst cattle
were mentioned Suffolk, Welsh, Devon and Hereford.

Oxen were still in some places used for ploughing. Pigs were of the Berkshire, Suffolk and Gloucester breeds.

The progress in the crops and stock had not been equalled by that in the employment of agricultural implements. Farmers still used "the great Hertfordshire wheel plough," an implement, according to Young, of "miserable construction." It required, as a rule, four horses or oxen harnessed abreast; and a driver besides the ploughman was, of course, necessary. Young urged the farmers to use something more up to date. He found a few farmers in the possession of threshing-machines worked by horses; they did not, however, seem to be very successful. A Bygrave farmer had a remarkable machine that cost him £400; it was worked by six horses, and threshed 25 to 30 loads of corn a day, ground wheat, cut chaff and dressed corn. Some farmers had a chaff-cutter, a turnip-slicer, an oil-cake mill, but they were rarities. Drills, though invented, as we have seen, a century before, were hardly at that time to be found in Hertfordshire, and Arthur Young clearly did not believe in them. He preferred "the common method of sowing broadcast." Of the few men whom he found employing drills, some horse-hoed their crops and claimed that they used less seed and kept their land cleaner than their neighbours.

There were six great turnpike roads running through this little county and also many good cross-roads. This made it easier for farmers to send their great four-horse waggons to London, taking straw, hay and wheat, and bringing back manure from the town. Other farmers would send to the great markets at Hertford and St. Albans, and there were doubtless also then as now good markets at Hitchin, Royston, Bishop's Stortford, Tring and Watford.

Here we see modern agriculture in its beginnings. Young remarked also on one feature which is peculiarly modern—an experiment in intensive culture, then being carried out by the Marchioness of Salisbury.

Although Young included in his book some information on the condition of labour, his description gave rural life as it appeared to the landlords and farmers.

The position of the other classes has also to be considered.

The larger villages must have contained then as now a considerable class intermediate between farmers and labourers. There were the village artisans, blacksmith, wheelwright, saddler and carpenter, the shoemaker and the tailor. These men, not having to face the sharp competition that subsequently sprang up, doubtless prospered more than did their successors in the latter years of the century. In the same rank of life were a few small shopkeepers and dealers. In addition there remained, in most places, some small holders, a remnant of the older life; these small men had lost or were losing the spinning, weaving and other industries which had supplemented their purely agricultural work, but where commons remained, they would usually have had rights of grazing for their stock, and many of the artisans would have the same advantages. All these people must have formed an independent class even in those days. Many of them were Nonconformists, Methodists perhaps, and often gave sympathy and support to the labourers, who formed the bulk of the population.

The artisans, small holders, etc.

The position of the labouring class was, in the early years of the century, deplorable. Save in special districts, where old industries such as weaving and spinning had survived, or new industries such as straw-plaiting or lace-making had sprung up, the men had to depend entirely on their low wages, supplemented, if they chose to become paupers, by allowances from the rates. Wages, though they varied then as now throughout the country, and were to some extent regulated by the Speenhamland regulations, seem to have averaged from 9s. to 10s. a week. Food was excessively dear. The whole labouring class must have lived on the verge of starvation. The more enterprising men poached and stole; they also joined with their fellows in rick-burnings, in the breaking-up of machinery, in the raiding of corn-stores, and in the other disorders that, taking place from time to time during the early years of the century, culminated in the risings of 1830. These disorders, though they may have paved the way both to political reforms and to the modification of the extraordinarily severe penal code, brought no immediate benefits to the people. The leaders, undoubtedly often the best of the men, were soon caught in the meshes of the law, to be transported or imprisoned until their spirit was broken. The less enterprising members of this class accepted their life of misery and learnt to depend on the allowances of the poor law and the doles they received from clergy and gentry. Amongst these poor people the population increased rapidly, all considerations of thrift being at an end, since the larger the families the more the labourers could secure from the rates. But even then some failed to secure enough

*The labourers and William Cobbett.*

to keep body and soul together and there were many
deaths from starvation.  Of those who became paupers,
some, especially the children, drifted into the parish
poorhouse, where, to quote a description given by Mr.
George Villiers, quoted by Arthur Young, were collected " the aged and infirm ; the dying and even the
dead ; the young and able, the abandoned and the
well-disposed ; modest want and indigent profligacy,
all confounded in one wretched mass."   Children
gathered from the poorhouses were formed into gangs
to be employed as ' apprentices ' in the factory towns
or to work under gangers in the fields.

It is interesting to compare the struggle which
continued for a generation at the beginning of the
XIXth century with the thirty years' struggle of the
XIVth century.   In the earlier period the fight was
carried on by a sturdy landholding peasantry, independent in mind and energetic in character, with
the tradition and habit of combined action and the
support of many well-wishers.  The peasants appear
to have been well organized, confident and capable.
But at the beginning of the XIXth century the main
part of the peasant class had sunk into a slough of
despond, and had no longer the sturdiness and
independence that had characterized their ancestors.
They had lost the habit of co-operating, whilst any
definite form of combination [1] was, until 1824, barred
by Act of Parliament.  Moreover, the labourers had
to face strong opposition : for the farmers had the
landed gentry and to some extent the clergy behind
them, and Parliament stood behind the landed gentry.
On the other hand, the labourers, unlike the peasants
of the XIVth century, had few sympathizers.  There

[1] See Appendix, p. 168.

is indeed only one man of marked distinction who supported the labourers with intelligence and understanding. This was William Cobbett. Cobbett, soldier, farmer and journalist, was born in 1762. His father was a Surrey farmer, his grandfather a labourer, and he began life on the land, like most country children of his time, employed in bird-scaring. After a few years of agricultural work, he left the country whilst still a lad to lead a life of adventure. Early in the XIXth century, when about forty years old, he returned from America, where he had been living for some years, and started a newspaper, which he ultimately carried on under the name of the *Political Register*. He soon became, thanks to his extraordinary energy and capacity as a speaker and writer, a great force in English political life. From 1821 onwards he made many expeditions throughout England on horseback, and the account of these wanderings, picturesquely told in his "Rural Rides," gives a picture of the human side of the rural life of the time, and does much to supplement Arthur Young's descriptions. After the passing of the Reform Act Cobbett was returned to Parliament, but at that time his health was failing, and he died in 1835. During the early years of the century, Cobbett's voice was constantly being raised to explain to the public the nature of the labourers' troubles, and to support them in their pitiable struggle: but even with his help, the forces against them were too strong, and the men seem to have actually lost ground, especially after 1812, when the scale of allowance from the rates began to be reduced and the pressure of poverty became more intense. But the spirit of the people was not entirely broken. In 1830 the labourers, to quote *The Times*, "exasperated into madness by insufficient food and clothing, by utter want of necessaries for themselves and their unfortunate families," were in open revolt. This revolt, which took the form of the gathering of the people into mobs, varying from a few hundred to a thousand or more, commenced towards the end of August of that year at Hardres in Kent, where some four hundred labourers collected together and destroyed some threshing-machines. The spread of threshing-machines had been a severe blow to the men. Winter threshing in the barns was comparatively well-paid work, and kept men occupied from late autumn to early spring; the introduction of machines made it possible for the farmers to dispense with this work and to dismiss their labourers after harvest, leaving them, perhaps, penniless to face the winter. The labourers' action had, it will be seen, some reason behind it. During the autumn the movement spread from east to west, and there were widespread disorders in Kent, Sussex, Surrey, Berkshire, Hampshire, Wiltshire and Gloucestershire, and to a less extent in almost all the other counties of England. The mobs demanded as a rule 2s. 6d. a day and regular employment. They destroyed many threshing-machines, and there was much rick-burning. Attacks were constantly made on overseers who had made themselves unpopular by their manner of administering the poor law, and in a few cases on other individuals, but as a rule the methods employed were orderly. *The Times* special correspondent says the "conduct of the peasantry has been admirable" : he describes how, when "a parish has risen," the men gave notice to the farmers, and appointed representatives, "sometimes a Methodist teacher," to treat with them. The farmers were generally frightened into agreeing to the demands, which were considered reasonable by independent persons. The magistrates at first sometimes acted as mediators.

There seemed every prospect that the movement might have ended in a definite improvement in the wages, and the conditions of life of the labouring population. But towards the end of November the government became frightened, and the lord-lieutenants and the magistracy were urged to proceed with greater vigour in quelling disturbances. The government's fright created a panic amongst the magistracy. Everywhere they took action : arbitrary arrests became common, and the gaols were soon crowded. The trials that followed were too often a mockery of justice. At Winchester some three hundred prisoners were tried in batches, and the evidence given was in many cases of a most shadowy kind ; in some instances it depended solely on the statements of informers, to whom large sums of money were given. Of the three hundred, over two hundred were found guilty of various offences ; of these about half were convicted of rioting and rick-burning and other similar crimes, for which in those days the penalty was death. Two of these men were hanged in the presence of the whole of the condemned men, and the remainder were transported or sentenced to hard labour. Similar repressive measures went on throughout the country. The movement among the labourers was crushed, and they were forced back into a silent poverty.

Two years later, at the time when the laws against combinations had been repealed, and there was a spread of trade unions throughout the towns, Hampshire men, following the example of their fellow-workers in the cities, formed a Labourers' Society and secured an advance in wages. Later, in 1834, some Dorset men of the village of Tolpuddle, where wages were 7s. a week, formed what they called a Friendly Society of Agricultural Labourers. The leaders were promptly clapped into prison and transported to Botany Bay, on the plea that they had administered unlawful oaths. As a protest against this action, a national agitation on a large scale, fostered and aided by the famous social reformer Robert Owen, was carried on for two years; the men were then pardoned and, ultimately, brought back to England. The very agitation and the publication of the facts showed to the governing class that arbitrary action would be from that time onward subject to national criticism, and this, perhaps, served as a wholesome check. On the other hand, this same agitation must have showed to the labouring population of rural England how powerless they were; it is not, therefore, surprising to find that the trade union movement obtained no hold on the villages for a period of about forty years.

At the beginning of the reign of Queen Victoria, conditions for farmers were improving. Rents had by then fallen considerably from the higher figures of the early years of the century, and so farmers definitely benefited by the prices that then prevailed. In 1836 the Tithe Commutation Act[1] had removed a farmers' grievance, and replaced the collections of the tenth on all 'growing and moving' things by a cash payment.

Progress in the early Victorian period.

[1] See Appendix, p. 176.

In 1838 the Royal Agricultural Society was founded, and its shows, continued ever since, have brought before landlords and farmers all the current improvements in both stock and machinery. A few years later systematic experiments in agriculture were started by Mr., afterwards Sir, John Lawes at his farm at Rothamsted, and scientific agriculture made a beginning. From Rothamsted, farmers have from that time been able to learn much of the exact value of manures, the best rotation of crops, and the principles which underlie the improvement of stock. Improvements in these matters and in other directions went slowly and steadily on year by year. Lighter ploughs were introduced, and there was a wider use of the threshing-machine and of the drill. Scientific methods of draining were introduced by Smith of Deanston, and cylindrical pipes made cheaply by machinery resulted in the spread of both deep and surface drainage. This had a great effect in bringing wet land under cultivation. Manuring was carried on upon more scientific lines, and nitrate of soda and guano began to be used for this purpose. Stock steadily improved, and crops increased in amount and were of better quality. In addition to other roots, mangel-wurzels and kohlrabi spread, and there was a more scientific growth and selection of seed of all sorts.

At first the improvements were only taken up by the larger farmers, but after the introduction of Free Trade in 1849 they spread more rapidly. The drop in prices which then occurred created a panic, and though the fall was only temporary in character, it seems to have caused agriculturists to bestir themselves to greater efforts. Good farming of the modern type then spread widely throughout England. The actual novelties introduced in the years that followed were few but important. The mowing and reaping machines enormously reduced harvest work. The elevators also saved labour. Moreover, the railways brought coal to the country to be used by steam-engines to drive threshing-machines ; this resulted in a further saving.

As the years passed hedges were cut down and the fields grew larger, whilst the same tendency affected the farms themselves, which were constantly being thrown together. Estates were also being enlarged, and in 1873 4,000 individuals owned more than half the land of England and Wales.

In 1834 the Poor Law Amendment Act[1] extended to the whole of England an arrangement already adopted in some districts, whereby parishes were grouped into 'Unions.' Each Union was to have its own workhouse, and was to be controlled by 'Guardians of the Poor' elected from the parishes. The old system of allowances was abolished by the same Act ; all able-bodied paupers who required relief had to come into the Union workhouse to be there set to work, whilst outdoor relief was provided for widows and the aged and others who could not be considered as able-bodied. Into the workhouses came not only a selection of the able-bodied but, as permanent inmates, a miscellaneous collection of unfortunate people, including pauper imbeciles and many pauper children.

The poor.

The system of responsibility of the parish for the paupers who had 'settled' within its boundaries continued after the act of 1834, and as a result there was still a tendency to get rid of cottages and take other

[1] See Appendix, p. 171.

steps to keep possible paupers outside the parish boundaries. However, by legislation [1] and government regulations the evils arising from the law of settlement were ultimately brought to an end, and from 1865 the Union, as a whole, and not the parish has been responsible for the poor, whilst a year's residence has been substituted for all other methods of obtaining a settlement.

The abolition in 1834 of the old system of allowances on which the labourer had learnt to depend, whilst it was intended to give him a new independence, at first depressed him into greater poverty, since his wages rarely rose in proportion to his losses. The labourer's remedy was to increase his income by keeping his wife and children at work in the fields. Women were generally employed in the dairy and in such work as weeding and hoeing; in some places they acted as carters, in others they even prepared and loaded manure. The use of women's labour became almost universal. Many of the women, including quite young girls, also worked in the large mixed gangs which were common at this period; the evils connected with these gangs were so great that they were regulated by legislation,[2] and ultimately were given up in most parts of England.

**The labourers.**

As the decades passed there was a slight increase in labourers' wages, but it was not sufficient to tempt men of enterprise to stay in the villages. As a result, during all this period of forty years a great migration from the country went on, and men of energy and ability, instead of staying in rural England to struggle against overwhelming difficulties, drifted away to the

[1] See Appendix, p. 171.       [2] Ibid. p. 168.

towns and colonies; the women followed. Probably this exodus of the best people—the natural leaders—was the cause of the final disappearance of the old co-operative and social life. All that had survived of the festivals and merrymakings so characteristic of English rural life in the past was disappearing during these years, whilst the great fairs also decayed. Indeed, by the end of the period little social life remained save the harvest home, the club day of the village sick and benefit society, and such meetings of friends as occurred at the country towns on market days.

In the North of England the conditions were somewhat different. There was a considerable improvement in wages, which, in 1870, in some counties, were over 16s. a week. It was this increase that encouraged the labourers in their final struggle. This struggle, of which the immediate cause was their desperate condition during the exceptionally hard winter of 1871–2, was led by Joseph Arch. Arch, born in 1828, was the son of a labourer; he had himself started life on the land at nine years old, employed in bird-scaring, standing, as he describes himself, "in a new-sown field shivering for twelve hours a day on an empty stomach, whilst the cold wind blew and chill rain poured down in torrents." At ten he was a ploughboy, at sixteen a mower at 1s. 6d. a day, working from 5 a.m. to 7 p.m. As he grew up he soon showed himself a man of considerable ability, won a gold medal for hedging and ditching, and became a contractor on a small scale for agricultural work. He travelled much in this capacity. He was also a Nonconformist preacher, and later on showed himself to be a convincing speaker. He was a man of what in these days would be called moderate views, and he secured considerable support from men of all classes.

The movement with which Arch's name is associated started on the 7th of February, 1872, at a meeting at Wellesbourne in Warwickshire. The word 'had been passed round,' says Arch, and some two thousand men had collected round an old chestnut-tree. Arch, standing on an old ' pig stool,' addressed the men. The outcome of this meeting was the spread of Trade Unionism throughout rural England and the formation of a Federation—the National Agricultural Labourers' Union —which at one time represented at least 80 thousand men. The Union demanded a wage of 16s. a week for labourers, 1s. a week more than had been asked for and very generally promised in 1830. A widespread agitation was conducted throughout England. Month after month and year after year Arch and his associates held their meetings throughout the counties, encouraging the men of the scattered villages to stand together for their common cause. They encountered bitter hostility amongst a large section of the landed gentry, the clergy and the farmers, the last of whom formed counter-organizations to resist the labourers' demands. But still they went steadily on. Strikes and lock-outs were common features of the movement, and the Union also emigrated many thousands of labourers to the colonies, and transferred others from one part of the country to another. Although the Labourers' Union secured no dramatic successes, there was, as the result of its work, a general rise in wages amounting to 1s. to 4s. a week. The movement lost much of its strength after the agricultural catastrophe that occurred about 1879.

There were three other features of the time affecting labourers' lives that require consideration. Poaching, which had been to a previous generation not only a source of food but also a source of wealth, decreased as risks increased. This increase of risk arose from the systematic employment of gamekeepers and the improved organization of the police, to whom new and increased powers were given.[1] Further, the enclosure of a large part of the remaining commons then took place, depriving many labourers of the remnants of their grazing rights, while this class suffered greatly from the bad state of the cottages, and also from a want of allotments, though in some places, in response to widespread agitation, small plots of land were provided for labourers.

The power of the country gentry in Parliament was greatly weakened by the Reform Act of 1832,[2] which brought into the House of Commons a large body of men of the commercial classes. But the local control of the country-side remained for long in the hands of the squirearchy, who from quarter and petty sessions continued to administer rural England. The main change in the form of local government was the decay of the rural parish as a controlling power, on the administration of the poor law[3] and, in some districts of the roads, passing into the hands of the Guardians of the Poor and Highway Boards[4] respectively.

**Central and local government.**

The Anglican Church had by the beginning of the XIXth century grown out of touch with the views and

[1] See Appendix, p. 172.  [2] Ibid. p. 167.
[3] Ibid. p. 171.  [4] Ibid. p. 174.

ideas of such of the peasantry as remained, and of the labourers who represented the old peasant class. The

**The Church and Dissent.** country parson had none of the characteristics of the village priest of the Middle Ages. He was, indeed, in his social status above even the leaseholding farmers, and, as a rule, squires and parsons ranked together, meeting on terms of social equality. The poorer parsons, and there were many very poor benefices, were tied to their homes, and here they devoted their spare time to some attractive hobby such as archaeology or natural history. But the men with private property or richer benefices took an active part in country life. They attended the social functions of the gentry, often shot and sometimes hunted with them, and took part in other forms of sport. Some sat on the Boards of Guardians, many were magistrates. Such men belonged to the governing class, and many indeed held what was called the 'family living.' Sometimes the parson was himself the squire, and so earned the nickname of 'squarson.' The typical country parson of the XIXth century was above all things a 'gentleman.' In religious matters he kept clear of the controversies of the time, avoiding fervour and adopting the moderate view, whilst in political life he supported, as a rule, the squire's party. Thus inspired, he took a friendly interest in the farmers, their wives and families, and in a kindly if somewhat patronizing spirit did something by the administration of doles to alleviate the miserable condition of the impoverished labourers. But when the labourers showed independence and made a struggle for better conditions, the parsons rarely actively supported them.

The influence of the Nonconformists was of a distinctly different character. The chapels of the more important sects, the Congregationalists, the Baptists and Methodists, were as a rule in the country towns or the big villages, and had the support of a section of the shopkeepers, a few of the more broad-minded farmers, and some of the village artisans and more intelligent labourers. Amongst these people the minister moved, definitely cut off by his religious views from the houses of the gentry, the clergy and the orthodox farmers. Such of the labourers as took an independent line in religion tended, if the opportunity offered, to attach themselves to the Primitive Methodists—the Ranters as they were often called. This offshoot of Methodism, founded early in the XIXth century, was, from its beginning, a movement led by rough, uneducated men, who made their appeal to the poor. Its preachers, like the mediaeval friars, were to be found tramping through the country districts preaching, in the face of much persecution, a gospel of simple Christianity. Many labourers became 'Primitives,' and their little chapels, built in the last century, are still common in some counties, especially in the East of England, where they had a strong following. The 'Primitives' have always shown sympathy with the labouring population. In 1830 they took an active part in the risings of that time, and in common with other Nonconformists did much to help the Trade Union movement in the 'seventies. Many of the leaders of the latter movement had, indeed, obtained their power of speaking through the practice they had obtained as local preachers.

All through the century the growth of business and trade and of social intercourse amongst the people continued. This growth served, in the early years of the century, to crowd the roads with waggons and with pack-horses, with cattle and stock of every description, with coaches and post-chaises, and individual travellers and parties on horseback or on foot. It **Roads and railways.** is not, therefore, surprising that the demand for better roads persisted. The government, anxious to get something done, put pressure on the turnpike trusts, and, under the direction of Telford and Macadam and their followers, good hard main roads continued to be constructed throughout England. On these roads, in the first half of the century, ran the swift mail-coaches that took passengers and the news of the world to the country towns of England. Such towns as were coaching centres flourished. Their inns became famous, their markets gained an additional importance, and the towns themselves became the centres of social life.

Meanwhile the greater number of the by-roads, which lay outside the operations of the trusts, remained very much in their old conditions; Parliament endeavoured to relieve the parishes of their responsibility, and to replace them by Highway Districts,[1] with Boards of management for such roads as lay outside the turnpike trusts. Later on turnpike trusts were gradually dissolved,[2] the Highway Boards or parishes taking over the duties: thus the system was by degrees abolished, the last turnpike being removed in the year 1895.

The importance of the roads for transit of goods and travellers was, of course, lessened with the growth of the railway system in the second half of the century; and the country lost much of the social life that centred round the great highways and the coaching inns. But the railways had their effect in the increase of trade and ease of travel; they helped to create a social life of a new character, and ultimately did much to destroy

[1] See Appendix, p. 174.        [2] Ibid. pp. 173, 174.

the old element of isolation which had been the characteristic of the English village from remote times.

Notwithstanding railways and new commercial ideas, sport maintained its position in rural life. Fox-hunting became more and more a great affair carried **Sport.** on at considerable cost. The coursing of hares continued. Shooting on a large scale spread throughout England, and every landholder of any importance had his gamekeeper. Enormous numbers of partridges and pheasants were preserved. Although an Act of Parliament, passed in 1831,[1] did away with the monopoly of killing game previously enjoyed by the large landholders, still shooting, like hunting and coursing, remained in the hands of the landholding and farming classes and such of the wealthy people of the towns as took a special interest in country life.

A sanguine student of rural life in the early 'seventies might have felt a real pride in describing rural England of the day. He could comment on the **Conclusion.** marvellous progress in cultivation and the reward obtained by the farmers for their capacity and energy. He could call attention to the real improvement in the condition of the labouring class since the early years of the century, when pauperism was almost universal amongst this class. He would have no doubts as to the success of the policy of 'enclosure,' of large farms, and of agriculture under Free Trade, and would feel himself justified in predicting a long period of prosperity on the lines laid down in the preceding half-century. Nothing would have suggested to him the possibility of the disaster that as a fact occurred.

[1] See Appendix, p. 172.

# CHAPTER X

## THE FINAL PHASE

AFTER 1875, the period of prosperity drew rapidly to a close. For several years the crops suffered from long spells of bad weather. Then in 1879 came **The agricultural disaster.** an epidemic of sheep-rot, which resulted in the destruction of millions of sheep. Foot and mouth disease was also prevalent, especially in 1883, when it attacked cattle and sheep and pigs on a large scale. There was also a drop in the price of corn, of butter and cheese, and, after 1885, of cattle and sheep. The fall in the price of corn continued owing to the large surplus crops in the United States, coupled with the improved transit arrangements which made the importation cheap and easy. During the twenty years 1880 to 1900 wheat averaged about 33s. a quarter; in 1894 the average of the recorded market prices actually dropped to 22s. 10d. a quarter, whilst in some places it was, on occasions, below £1 a quarter. The farmers also suffered from the difficulty of obtaining child labour, since the Education Act of 1876[1] kept the boys and girls at school. Women were also difficult to obtain, since the country girl, rather than work in the fields, went into service or into employment in the shops of the towns. Losses were enormous.

[1] See Appendix, p. 168.

In the years between 1876 and 1886 the annual income of the three classes interested in agriculture was estimated by Sir James Caird to have diminished by £42,800,000. But the hard times were not then over : from 1891 to 1894 repeated spells of bad weather went far to destroy the crops. Many farmers were ruined, and others, seeing no prospects before them, gave up their farms in order to migrate to the towns or to the colonies. Some land went out of cultivation, and of that which remained much was diverted from corn land to pasture. This conversion has continued until the beginning of the war, about one-fifth of the thirteen million acres devoted to corn in 1880 being then in pasture. Enterprising farmers here and there found remedies for their difficulties : some turned their attention, with success, to the production of fruit and vegetables, whilst others, by the use of self-binders and other improved machines, saved labour, and so expense. The position of their class was rendered somewhat easier by the fall of rents, and when the rise of prices came in the early years of the XXth century farmers began to do better.

This agricultural catastrophe produced a widespread discontent, and many remedies were suggested. On the one hand there was a demand for the **Remedies suggested and adopted.** reintroduction of the Corn Laws, whilst another class of thinkers asked, like the peasants of the XIVth and XVth centuries, for fixity of tenure, or at least full compensation for improvements effected by tenants. Some reformers urged that a partial remedy for the farmers' troubles would be found in co-operation, whilst the labourers and those who represented their views urged the State to interfere to increase the number of allotments and small holdings, and thus reconstruct the old system under which every countryman who needed it should have a plot of land. This turmoil of talk had some effect. Parliament had already in 1875 legislated on the question of compensation for improvements, and more effective statutes were subsequently passed.[1] The question of increasing the number of small holdings was also brought before Parliament in 1885, to be shelved for over twenty years, during which time the landlords and farmers continued, as they had done in the past, to incorporate small plots into the larger farms.

The position of settled estates was also considered, and legislation was carried which made it comparatively easy for such property to be sold.[2] Parliament also gave to agricultural tenants the right to kill the ground game,[3] relieved them of one half the rates on their land,[4] and placed the responsibility for the payment of tithe on their landlords.[4]

The labourers' organizations had been greatly weakened by the agricultural catastrophe. Thereupon the leaders, seeing no chance of increase of wages, **The labourers and their trade unions.** put their best energy into a demand for allotments and also joined in an agitation for the extension of the Parliamentary suffrage to labourers. It was in part the result of this agitation that the franchise was extended in 1884[5] to householders in the counties. In the following year Arch was returned to Parliament for a division of Norfolk. The Union, though much weakened, continued for many years; its successor, founded in 1906, exists

[1] See Appendix, p. 175.      [2] Ibid. p. 176.
[3] Ibid. p. 172.      [4] Ibid. p. 176.      [5] Ibid. p. 167.

at the present day, and appears to be rapidly spreading through England.

The control that the country gentry had exercised over Parliament, at which a blow had been struck by the Reform Act of 1832, was further **Central and local government.** weakened at the election of 1885, when in many counties the newly enfranchised labourers refused to vote for the landed proprietors of the old school or their representatives ; they returned to Parliament men of a different type belonging to the Liberal and Radical groups, whom they deemed to be more sympathetic to the views of their class. Though there has been some reaction to this revolt, the political influence of the country gentry has been permanently weakened. A similar change took place in local government when Parliament intervened to transfer the management of country affairs from the justices of the peace to elected county councils, district councils, parish councils and parish meetings.[1]

The employment of these bodies by Parliament in the reconstruction of conditions of life in rural England has created what is perhaps the most interesting feature of their work. The management of the main roads,[2] the organization of education,[3] and the creation of small holdings[3] has been entrusted to the county councils; the care of the secondary roads[2] and the supervision and even building of labourers' cottages, a great need in many parts of England, to the district councils ;[4] and the provision of allotments to the parish councils and meetings.[3] Under this control an admirable system of roads has at last been created throughout England, and

[1] See Appendix, p. 167.
[2] Ibid. p. 174.
[3] Ibid. p. 175.
[4] Ibid. p. 174.

an important educational system has been built up ;
but the policy of providing small holdings and labourers'
cottages has not, as a rule, been sufficiently actively
pressed to make our country-side attractive to the more
energetic young men and women of the labouring class,
and the migration to the towns and colonies has continued.

Rural life was very different at the time of the beginning of the war from what it had been forty years before.
**Social changes.** In the agricultural catastrophe it was the
old-fashioned squires and farmers who dis-
appeared, and the men who took their place,
many of whom came from the towns to buy land from
the half-ruined landlords, have rarely been imbued with
the autocratic spirit of their predecessors. Education,
in all its aspects, had spread ; as a result there was
more tolerance. The same spirit animated the religious
world, although the Anglican parson was still inclined
to stand by the gentry, and continued to take social
precedence of the Nonconformist minister. Even the
farmers, though more inclined than squire and parson
to cling to the old point of view, were influenced by
the new spirit, whilst the new market-gardeners to
be found in almost all parts of England were eager
for new ideas and new methods. Moreover, many
manufactories were erected along the railway lines, and
men of all classes had come out from towns to settle
down in the country and influence its life. Amongst
the labourers there was still much poverty ; the houses
were often miserable, while in many districts small plots
of land were difficult to obtain. But although the men
were still, in old-fashioned neighbourhoods, often subject
to a personal control which they found extremely irksome
and often bitterly resented, there was little of the degra-

dation that marked the life of the XIXth century. Moreover, the labourer was protected under the provisions of
recent legislation in case of accidents [1] and of sickness.[2]

There were many new and hopeful elements in rural
life. The co-operative movement in agriculture, fostered
by the Agricultural Organization Society, was spreading
throughout England and drawing all classes together.
Farmers were showing increasing energy and ability.
The new small holders, living on the great estates of
the county councils, were successfully building up under
favourable conditions a type of life new to England.
At the same time elementary education, compulsory
and also free to all,[3] supplemented by opportunities for
secondary education,[3] in both agricultural and intellec-
tual subjects, had created a widespread intelligence and
a new social life was arising. Village club-rooms, with
newspapers and libraries, were common throughout
England. Dancing, music and acting were being reintroduced, and were taken up by all classes working
together. In villages imbued with the modern spirit the
labourer was no longer a drudge, with no views outside
his work. He studied his weekly paper and took an
interest in national politics. Even if he had not himself,
at some period of his life, been away from his home to
work in towns or colonies, he would have friends all
over the world from whom he heard from time to time.
Thus he obtained a broader outlook on life. His wife
and children were not behind him in intelligence.

Even before the outbreak of the great war, the
remnants of the bastard feudalism that, arising in the
XVIIIth century, had done so much harm to our village
life was rapidly dissolving. There was a widespread
feeling that we were at the beginning of a new era.

[1] See Appendix, p. 168.    [2] Ibid. p. 176.    [3] Ibid p. 175.

Davena
statistics
that 55 pe
The amoi
small. W
acres in I
or pasture
cultivatioi
fifths wou
Judging
of the XI
cultivatioi
is now, of
follow tha
been defii
the XVII
(6 million
remaining
by agreer
who boug
of ownerl
The gro
middle o
undoubte
land by lo
enclosure
There
large area
character
considera
woods, su
rights. A
closed ar
parishes
at Soham
There ar
doubtless
learn tha
provision

# APPENDIX

## PART I

### A. *The Tùn, the Vill and the Parish*

ENGLISH country people have, from very early times, been grouped into small communities, living in definite areas. Before the Norman Conquest the area was called the 'tùn'; this word means a wall or boundary and was in the first instance applied to the fenced-in settlements. After the Conquest the word 'tùn,' modified into 'town,' continued for centuries to be applied to the village and the area of land that went with it, and the word is employed in the old sense in New England to-day. At the same time a new title, the 'vill,' came into use.

Later, in the XVIth century, and perhaps before that time, the civil parish is the unit. The 'vill' may be described as the direct descendant of the 'tùn,' but the parish is, of course, a very old division, created by the Church, into which the vill seems to have merged, giving the parish a double character, civil and ecclesiastical.

The words 'tùn' and 'vill,' like 'parish,' are also often applied to the community itself.

The powers and duties of the communities varied from time to time, but the characteristic features were these :—

1. The democratic transaction of business in open meeting, the tùn-moot of Saxon times, the town's meeting of a later period, then the vestry, and finally the parish meeting of to-day.

2. The election of special officers for the management of such affairs as the community had to deal with.

3. A right to levy rates and taxes either for local expenses, or to provide an amount levied on the community by a superior authority.

### B. *Socage Tenants*

From the XIIIth century onwards free tenants, other than those who held by military tenure, were known as 'socage tenants' or 'tenants in socage.' On estates that were or had

### E. *Agricultural Rents in Modern Times*

The variation of agricultural rents in England in modern times is a matter on which contemporary writers have from time to time made comments and estimates, from which it is possible to draw some general conclusions. In 1790, 10s. to 12s. an acre appears to have been an ordinary rent; then a rise began which continued until 1812, when the average may have been as high as 50s. an acre. The rise was followed by an almost equally rapid drop, until in 1830 the average was probably as low as 20s. The tide then turned again, and rents went up steadily until 1879, when the average was about 35s. Then followed a drop of about 30 per cent., and by the close of the century the 35s. an acre had fallen to 25s. Since then there has been very little change, though there was a definite tendency for rents to rise during the years that immediately preceded the war.

Students must use these figures with discretion, for they have to be considered in relation, not only to the character of the buildings and the capital sunk by landlord or tenant in the land, but also with reference to the liability for rates, taxes and tithe. It must be remembered, for example, that whilst a century ago the tenant provided tithe and paid heavy rates and taxes, at the present time the landlord pays the tithe, the rates are reduced under the provisions of the Agricultural Rates Act (see below, p. 176), whilst the tenant is usually free from any liability for income tax.

## PART II

#### ACTS OF PARLIAMENT AND A ROYAL ORDINANCE REFERRED TO IN THE TEXT, AND SOME OTHER SELECTED STATUTES, WITH SOME NOTES THEREON.

*THE STATUTES AT LARGE, from Magna Carta onwards, edited by Danby Pickering, were published in book form in 1762; supplementary volumes continued the collection of statutes until 1807. Subsequently the statutes have been published officially.*

*In a few cases, where authorities attribute different years of the calendar to a statute, both dates are given.*

*The quotations from statutes given in the text are sometimes abbreviated.*

## I. STATUTES RELATING TO GOVERNMENT AND RIGHT OF VOTING AT PARLIAMENTARY ELECTIONS

## II. STATUTES, ETC., RELATING TO WAGES AND OTHER LABOUR QUESTIONS

## III. STATUTES RELATING TO ENCLOSURES

(Also see below, p. 169.)

## IV. STATUTES RELATING TO DEPOPULATION, TILLAGE, AND ENCLOSURE PASSED IN THE XVTH AND XVITH CENTURIES

*All the statutes given below follow the same general lines (see p. 84). They are of special interest from the descriptions of rural conditions set out in the recitals of the acts.*

## V. POOR LAW STATUTES

## VI. THE GAME LAWS

## VII. STATUTES RELATING TO IMPORTATION AND EXPORTATION OF CORN

1815 **55 George III, c. 26.**—Directed that wheat could not be imported from North American colonies at under 67s. per quarter, nor from elsewhere at under 80s. per quarter, and made similar rules for other corn ... ... 135

1828 **9 George IV, c. 60.** ⎫—Created sliding scales of
1842 **5 & 6 Victoria, c. 14.** ⎬ import duties varying with prices, instead of a fixed rate ... ... ... ... 135

1846 **9 & 10 Victoria c. 22.**—Reduced import duties on corn, as from 1st February, 1849, to 1s. per quarter ... 135

1869 **32 & 33 Victoria c. 14.**—Cancelled the 1s. per quarter duty.


## VIII. STATUTES RELATING TO ROADS AND BRIDGES

1530 **22 Henry VIII, c. 5.**—Enacted that where liability for repairing bridges could not be attached to any existing authority or person, the maintenance of bridges, if outside the towns, should be undertaken by the counties : quarter sessions were empowered to administer the law and make a county rate for the purpose ... ... ... ... ... ... ... 90

1555 **2 & 3 Philip & Mary, c. 8.**—Provided that the parishes should be responsible for the maintenance of the highways ... ... ... ... ... ... ... 91

1663 **15 Carolus II, c. 1.**—Authorized the setting up of toll bars at certain points on the Great North Road ... 105

About From the middle of the XVIIth century and all
1650 through the XVIIIth, statutes were being passed
to through Parliament regulating the size of cartwheels,
1800 the number of horses to be harnessed to waggons, etc. 120

1706 From 1706 onwards, thousands of Acts of Parliament
to were passed creating Turnpike Trusts. Under these
1895 acts a certain number of persons were appointed to make and maintain a specific piece of road and were given powers to levy tolls for this purpose. These powers were limited to a definite period, and when the period expired Parliament was applied to for a renewal. In the XVIIIth century and the first half of the XIXth

PAGE

century these renewals were usually granted. I have been unable to ascertain when new trusts cease to be created ; but, it appears, that from 1864 onwards, the system was somewhat discredited : renewals became rare. As a result the trusts gradually expired, whilst some were specifically abolished. The last trusts expired in 1895 ... ... ... ... ... 120, 125

1835 5 & 6 William IV, c. 50.⎫ —These and some other
1858 21 & 22 Victoria, c. 98.⎪ statutes were passed in the
1862 25 & 26 Victoria, c. 61.⎬ XIXth century, directed
1863 26 & 27 Victoria, c. 17.⎪ towards depriving the
1878 41 & 42 Victoria, c. 77.⎭ parishes of the responsibility for the repair of the roads, and vesting it in Highway Boards. The statutes only came into effective operation in certain parts of England, possibly in one half ... ... ... ... ... ... 152, 155

1888 51 & 52 Victoria, c. 41.—Local Government Act : placed the management of the main roads in the hands of the County Councils ... ... ... ... ... 160

1894 56 & 57 Victoria, c. 73.—Local Government Act : placed the management of roads other than main roads in the hands of the District Councils ... ... ... 160

*The complicated legislation relating to roads and bridges can be best studied from "The Story of the King's Highway," by Sidney and Beatrice Webb (Longmans).*

## IX. STATUTES RELATING TO HOUSING, SMALL HOLDINGS, ETC.

1589 31 Elizabeth, c. 7.—Enacted (1) that no one was to build a cottage or convert a building into a cottage for workers on the land without allotting to it 4 acres of land, and (2) that two families were not to occupy one cottage. This act was repealed in 1775 ... ... 84

1890 53 & 54 Victoria, c. 70.⎫ —Under the provisions of
1909 9 Edward VII, c. 44. ⎭ these acts, cottages in rural districts, as well as in towns, are subject to inspection. The Rural District Council concerned has power to order the landlord to put unhealthy cottages into sanitary condition and to build new cottages ... ... 160

1907 7 **Edward VII**, c. 54. ⎫ —Under these acts (the
1908 8 **Edward VII**, c. 36. ⎭ second being a consolidatory act), the County Councils are directed to provide small holdings, and the Parish Councils allotments for suitable applicants ... ... ... ... ... ... 160

*There was some previous legislation in the XIXth century on the question of allotments.*

## X. STATUTES RELATING TO EDUCATION

1870 33 & 34 **Victoria**, c. 75.—Directed that England was to be portioned out into school districts, and schools for elementary education provided at public expense under school boards wherever needed.

1876 39 & 40 **Victoria**, c. 79.—Laid down the principle that every parent had to see that his child received an elementary education : and limited employment of children (see above, p. 168) ... ... ... ... 157

1891 54 & 55 **Victoria**, c. 56.—Abolished school fees for Elementary Education ... ... ... ... ... 161

1902 2 **Edward VII**, c. 42.—Transferred administration of elementary education to County Councils, and gave Councils power to provide facilities for secondary education ... ... ... ... ... ... 160, 161

1906 6 **Edward VII**, c. 57.—Authorized the provision of free meals for poor children.

## XI. STATUTES RELATING TO IMPROVEMENTS EFFECTED BY AGRICULTURAL TENANTS

1875 38 & 39 **Victoria**, c. 92.—A non-compulsory act ... 159

1883 46 & 47 **Victoria**, c. 61.—Gave tenant farmers compensation for certain improvements ... ... ... 159

1908 8 **Edward VII**, c. 28.—Consolidated the law and somewhat extended the rights of farmers and market gardeners in relation to compensation for improvements, etc.

## XII. SUNDRY STATUTES

# INDEX

*The Appendix is not indexed in detail; all Acts of Parliament referred to in the text appear in the Appendix, Part II, and are accordingly omitted from this index. The letters f. and ff. indicate the page or pages following the preceding number.*

*Printed in Great Britain by*

UNWIN BROTHERS, LIMITED, THE GRESHAM PRESS, WOKING AND LONDON